W9-CHW-684

toasted

toasted

THE NEW
TOASTER OVEN
COOKBOOK

MARIA HAUSCHEL

whitecap

Copyright © 2002 by Maria Hauschel
Whitecap Books

All rights reserved. No part of this publication may be reproduced,
stored in a retrieval system, or transmitted in any form or by any
means, electronic, mechanical, photocopying, recording or otherwise, without prior written consent of the publisher.

The information contained in this book is not intended to replace
your toaster oven manual or the manufacturer's recommendations.
The author and publisher disclaim any and all liability incurred in
connection with the use of information and recipes in *Toasted*. For
additional information, please contact Whitecap Books Ltd.
351 Lynn Avenue, North Vancouver, BC V7J 2C4.

Edited by Elaine Jones
Proofread by Lesley Cameron
Cover design and illustration by Don Bull
Photography by Derik Murray
Front cover photograph and ovens in interior photographs courtesy of DeLonghi
Food styling by Joanne Facchin
Interior design by Tanya Lloyd Kyi

Printed and bound in Canada.

NATIONAL LIBRARY OF CANADA CATALOGUING IN PUBLICATION DATA
Hauschel, Maria.
   Toasted

   Includes index.
   ISBN 1-55285-213-X

   1. Toaster oven cookery. I. Title.
TX840.T63H38 2002   641.5'86   C2002-910192-1

The publisher acknowledges the support of the Canada Council and
the Cultural Services Branch of the Government of British Columbia in
making this publication possible. We acknowledge the financial
support of the Government of Canada through the Book Publishing
Industry Development Program for our publishing activities.

contents

acknowledgements

Putting together a cookbook takes so much more than just an author providing the recipes. It would not have been possible without the efforts of a team of very special people. My sincere thanks go to:

Robert, Robin, Roberta, Angela and Claire at Whitecap for their patience and professionalism throughout.

Elaine Jones, my dedicated recipe editor, for her enthusiastic encouragement.

Don Bull, of Don Bull Creative, for his outstanding cover design and putting up with just one more suggestion.

Joanne Facchin, the multi-talented food stylist and chef, who has enormous patience and perfect presentation. You are a goddess.

Stephen Wong at MOTIV and Tanya Roland at Country Furniture for supplying such beautiful props for the photographs.

I'm extremely thankful to my wonderful mother, Beth, who taught me, inspired me, encouraged me and shared with me her passion for food and the joy of cooking. To my dad, Mike, who dutifully taste tested my mom's recipes and encouraged me at each stage of the process. I love you both.

Last, but definitely not least, to my talented, creative, dedicated and super supportive partner, Derik Murray. Without his love and attention to detail this project would not have been possible. Thank you for everything and so much more—especially for the beautiful photographs (that speak for themselves)—you didn't miss a beat! You're a type A but you're the still the best.

introduction

"it uses less energy but heats up quickly"

"start small, but start cooking"

"perfect for the student, single professional
or couples young and old"

"get inspired! you never know where
your imagination will take you"

I WASN'T ALWAYS COMFORTABLE IN THE KITCHEN. For years my Mom encouraged me to take part, to learn and prepare the dishes she so effortlessly put together. I resisted mostly due to fear. I felt I would never be able to create the delicious food she so clearly could make with her eyes closed. But I did watch, and I also listened. There was really no choice.

My family's home is one where, even while you eat your meal you're already thinking and talking about the next one. This is not to say that we had a lot of time to devote solely to thinking about food! We were a small household, just us three, but with both my parents working and my second home being the ice rink—I was a competitive figure skater—we had to be organized. My parents are also of European heritage and so food for them is really about life. You live to eat, not the other way around. And good food means fresh food. There were no frozen dinners in our freezer.

When I finally ventured out on my own, I quickly understood just how much my parents knew about food, and I began to yearn for those home-cooked meals my mother made. Finally, my fear of cooking took a back seat to hunger. But if I was going to learn to cook, I didn't want to end up toiling in the kitchen to find myself facing the week with 10 leftover servings of the same thing.

One weekend, while home on a visit, I talked to my Mom about what I could prepare in my own small kitchen while keeping the effort to a minimum—I was, after all, single in the big city and I had places to go, people to see!

Mom pointed to her trusty toaster oven. "How do you think I'm able to make great food but not spend all my time in the kitchen?" she asked. Of course, a toaster oven! There's less mess, it uses less energy and you can make smaller portions. You can prepare delicious meals using a fraction of the effort needed with a conventional oven, making the whole process less intimidating!

Calls to my Mom became our catch-up time. Along with my Mom's tips for preparing my toaster oven recipes, we shared news on our daily experiences, updates on friends and discussions on when I was going to settle down with someone (some things you just can't escape!). Soon I was impressing friends with my prowess in the kitchen and later, when I met someone to "settle down" with, I wowed him with my ability to prepare almost anything in my toaster oven. Eventually, my Mom and I started swapping recipes. You could say it's become a family tradition.

I wrote this cookbook to share with you what I've learned about cooking with a toaster oven. Over time I've become accustomed to letting my taste buds be my guide and eyeballing the ingredients for the meal I'm preparing. And you can too. I've left some blank pages for notes at the end of each chapter in the hope that you will experiment with and personalize these recipes, noting your additions or substitutions. The more you cook with a toaster oven, the more you'll be comfortable experimenting. In most cases, the measurements and sizes I've given are a guide— if there's an amount of an herb or a spice that you just have to have, go for it! Substitutions are also possible. Out of lemons but have plenty of grapefruits? Try it! You don't need a pantry or fridge full of special ingredients, just the basic stuff you've probably got on hand right now and certainly nothing that you can't find in your local grocery store. But remember, fresh is best! So start small, but start cooking. You never know what new traditions you might create. Just don't forget to call your mother!

why use a toaster oven

· It uses less energy but it heats up quickly.
· There is less mess during cooking and it's a breeze to clean.
· It's an inexpensive appliance that you can use every day.
· It's portable, so you can take it with you to the cottage
  or cabin.
· It bakes like an oven, broils like a broiler, heats up leftovers
  and toasts any thickness of bread in less time than a conven-
  tional oven.
· In hot summer weather it doesn't heat up your whole kitchen.
· It's perfect for the student, single professional or couples
  young and old .

choosing a toaster oven

Most any toaster oven will do, especially if you're just
getting into the cooking experience. If you're about to try
roasting a whole chicken though, look for those ovens
that have a larger capacity. Otherwise, try to find one
that's within your budget and has the features you feel
you need.

A great list of manufacturers—DeLonghi (as pictured in
this book), Black and Decker, Krups and Cuisinart, to
name a few—make toaster ovens. And because they are
popular additions to modern kitchens, you can pretty
much find them at any department, home, kitchen or
hardware store. Many manufacturers are now incorporat-
ing premium toaster oven options such as a convection
feature, interior lights, porcelain enamel interiors and
even digital displays.

Prices can range from $50 for entry-level toaster ovens
to $350 for the temperature-sensitive, convection/
conventional toaster oven. If it's within your budget, I'd

go for one that costs $140 to $200. This should give you a model with the ability to prepare most things you'd want to try. The toaster oven market is now trending towards convection ovens. Cooking times for convection ovens are about 30% less than that of normal ovens, making the entire cooking experience so much more efficient.

Toaster ovens do share some standard features. When you're shopping for one, look for those that have easy to read on/off bake controls with temperature settings, including broil. And don't forget to take note of the on/off toaster control. It should include the feature of choosing the toast setting—light, medium or dark. The oven should also come with an oven pan, slotted broiler tray or drip pan (fits into the oven pan) and a removable toaster oven rack (sometimes with a handle to help pull the rack out when it's hot).

For the purpose of the recipes in this book, the oven tray I use is the one that came with my toaster oven. It is approximately $9\frac{1}{2}$ inches wide, 10 inches long and $1\frac{1}{2}$ inches deep. Use this size of pan unless otherwise specified.

The oven tray is used as both a baking dish and a casserole dish. Many toaster ovens can also accommodate smaller glass or ceramic baking dishes and you can now buy muffin tins that bake six muffins at a time, in a size that will fit most toaster ovens. Check your local store's kitchen department for other handy items, such as mini loaf pans, insulated mini-cookie sheets or mini pizza pans.

Lastly, always make sure you comparison shop when purchasing any appliance. And make sure you're getting what you paid for—when you unpack it, check to see if each item that was mentioned as included is actually there. You'd hate to have to run out to exchange or return your toaster oven just when you're about to get down to cooking!

simple basics to have on hand

The following list includes the basics I'd have in my kitchen if I were just starting out. The whole point is to have a great foundation to build on. With these items and the right piece of fish or meat you're well on your way to a great meal. (Note that any meat you freeze should be purchased fresh, and I prefer to use only fresh fish, never frozen, as I find the taste suffers once you freeze it.)

Of course, there's a multitude of ingredients out there and I encourage you to experiment with whatever takes your fancy. Next time you're in the grocery store have a good look around and see what's on the shelves and in the produce bins. Get inspired! You never know where your cooking imagination will take you!

stocking the pantry:
- salt
- pepper
- dried oregano
- Spike seasoning (or Mrs. Dash)
- Italian seasoning
- garlic
- granulated sugar
- all-purpose flour
- baking soda and powder
- honey
- canned whole plum tomatoes
- Italian crushed tomato sauce
- canned cannellini or navy beans
- olive oil

- crackers
- pasta (various shapes and sizes)
- balsamic vinegar
- breadcrumbs
- packages of nuts (walnuts, hazelnuts, sliced almonds, etc)
- potatoes
- onions
- resealable plastic bags
- foil

stocking the fridge
- lemons (and lots of them)
- oranges
- grapefruit
- mustard (rough or Dijon)
- ketchup
- olives (green and black)
- fruit preserves
- butter
- lettuce (butter, spring mix, etc.)
- sour cream (great in mashed potatoes)
- basil pesto
- cheeses (Parmigiano-Reggiano, feta, goat cheese and any others you enjoy)
- fresh herbs
- sun-dried tomatoes packed in olive oil
- tomatoes
- bell peppers
- eggs
- spinach
- meats (chicken, pork, ground meats, etc.)
- frozen filo pastry

appetizers

"let your tastebuds be your guide"

"so easy and absolutely delicious"

"velvety and zesty, it will leave
you begging for more!"

"so elegant but undeniably simple!"

basic bruschetta with pesto

SERVES 2

This is my standard bruschetta and it never fails to please. Bruschetta is a colorful and robust little flavor surprise and it's my favorite appetizer. I don't toast my bread slices first because I dislike the way they dry out and fall apart when biting down on these treats. You can turn bruschetta into a light meal by serving it with a fresh green salad. Slice the baguette across and you'll have lovely little appetizers. Slice the baguette on an angle for a longer cut and you'll make something more substantial but you'll have to cook them in two batches. Any remaining bruschetta mix can be kept in the fridge for up to one week.

1 medium tomato, finely chopped
1/2 small red onion, finely chopped
salt and ground black pepper to taste
1/4 cup (60 mL) olive oil
1 Tbsp. (15 mL) balsamic vinegar
1 clove garlic, minced
1 Tbsp. (15 mL) dried oregano
6 thin slices baguette
1/4 cup (60 mL) basil pesto
1 cup (240 mL) grated Parmigiano-Reggiano cheese

Preheat the oven on broil. Place the slotted tray in the baking dish.

Combine the tomato, onion, salt and pepper, oil, vinegar, garlic and oregano in a small bowl. Toss to mix and set aside while you prepare the baguette.

Spread pesto on one side of the bread slices. Place bread, pesto side up, on the slotted tray. Distribute the tomato mixture over each piece of bread. Top each slice with cheese. Broil for 10 minutes, until the cheese is melted and bubbly.

Serve immediately.

a bit about parmesan cheese:

Parmigiano-Reggiano, an aged, hard cheese from Italy, is considered the king of all Parmesan cheeses. It has a unique nutty flavor and beautifully complements the recipes that call for it here. It works well equally on its own, served with some fresh fruit and a glass of chilled white wine.

If you can't find the real thing, don't fret. Italy has its variations on Parmesan—Grand Padano is one—and there are a number of Parmesan cheeses produced by manufacturers from Canada and the United States that will stand up to the challenge.

mushroom bruschetta

SERVES 2

This mushroom mixture has a rich, "meaty" flavor enhanced by the balsamic vinegar. For fun, try experimenting with different varieties like shiitake, portobello, cremini or oyster mushrooms.

2 Tbsp. (30 mL) olive oil
½ medium-sized onion, finely chopped
15 medium-sized mushrooms, roughly chopped
½ cup (120 mL) balsamic vinegar
1 Tbsp. (15 mL) chopped fresh basil
salt and freshly ground black pepper to taste
6 thin slices baguette
1 cup (240 mL) grated Asiago cheese

Heat the olive oil in a medium size fry pan over medium heat. Add the onion and cook until translucent, about 3 to 4 minutes. Do not let it brown. Add the mushrooms and cook, stirring frequently, until all the moisture has evaporated, about 7 minutes. Add the vinegar and continue to cook over medium heat, stirring frequently, until the liquid is reduced by half. This should take about 7 to 10 minutes. Remove from the heat and stir in the basil, salt and pepper.

Preheat the oven on broil. Place the bread slices on the slotted tray in the baking dish. Distribute the mushroom mixture evenly over the bread. Sprinkle the cheese evenly over top. Broil for 10 minutes, until the cheese is melted and bubbly. Serve immediately.

pesto gorgonzola bruschetta

This variation is my partner's absolute favorite. The creaminess of the Gorgonzola pairs well with the bite of the sun-dried tomato and the intensity of the basil pesto. I once happened to come upon arugula pesto and it was terrific as a substitute to the basil pesto. Sun-dried tomatoes in oil can be purchased julienne style. If you can't find them, use 4 whole sun-dried tomatoes in oil and slice each into 3 pieces.

³/₄ cup (60 mL) basil pesto
6 thin slices baguette
²/₃ cup (170 g) Gorgonzola cheese
12 slices of sun-dried tomato (packed in olive oil)

Preheat the oven on broil. Place the slotted tray in the oven dish.

Spread pesto over one side of the bread slices. Place the bread on the slotted tray. Crumble the cheese into 12 pieces. Place 2 pieces of cheese on each piece of bread. Place 2 slices of sun-dried tomato on each slice. Broil for 10 minutes, until the cheese is melted. Serve immediately.

olive walnut bruschetta

SERVES 2

Olive walnut pesto is also known as a tapenade. The mild nutty flavor of olives is greatly enhanced by the addition of walnuts.

6 thin slices baguette
½ cup (120 mL) olive walnut pesto
½ cup (120 mL) coarsely chopped walnuts
1 cup (225 g) grated Parmigiano-Reggiano cheese

Preheat the oven on broil. Place the slotted tray in the baking dish.

Spread walnut pesto on one side of the bread slices. Place the bread on the tray. Distribute the walnuts evenly over each slice of bread. Top each slice with cheese. Broil for 10 minutes, until the cheese is melted and bubbly. Serve immediately.

olive walnut pesto:

Olive walnut spread can be found in bulk at almost any Italian deli counter that carries an assortment of olives or in the gourmet food section of specialty grocers. If you can't locate it, you can make your own.

To make the pesto, combine ½ cup (120 mL) of finely chopped pitted olives (black or green), ½ cup (120 mL) of finely ground walnuts, 2 Tbsp. (30 mL) olive oil, 1 minced garlic clove and ¼ cup (120 mL) of finely ground Parmigiano-Reggiano cheese. Purée in the blender for 30 seconds and add salt and freshly ground black pepper to taste.

roasted eggplant bruschetta

Eggplant, roasted with balsamic vinegar, creates a rustic look and adds intense flavor to this bruschetta. I prefer the European varieties of eggplant over Asian, but let your tastebuds be your guide.

Serves 2

6 thin slices baguette
½ cup (120 mL) basil pesto sauce
6 slices roasted eggplant, roughly chopped (see page 62)
1 cup (225 g) grated mozzarella cheese

Preheat the oven to broil. Place the slotted tray in the baking dish.

Spread the pesto evenly on one side of each bread slice. Place the bread on the tray. Top each piece with eggplant. Sprinkle the grated mozzarella over each slice. Broil for 10 minutes, until the cheese is melted and bubbly. Serve immediately.

toasted antipasto

SERVES 4

Drawing from some of the roasted vegetable dishes in this section you can create a lovely platter of antipasto like the Italians do. Let your own favorites be your guide. Use a unique serving dish for added impact—something hand-painted like they'd use in Italy—and you've got the perfect start to an Italian-inspired evening. Some crusty fresh bread makes a nice addition.

4 slices roasted eggplant (see page 62)
6 pieces roasted onion (see page 63)
4 slices roasted zucchini (see page 66)
4 slices roasted red pepper (see page 61)
4 slices roasted yellow pepper (see page 61)
6 black Kalamata olives
6 large pieces, about 1-inch (2.5-cm) square, of
    Parmigiano-Reggiano cheese
3 Tbsp. (45 mL) balsamic vinegar

Make the roasted vegetables ahead of time and refrigerate them. Assemble all the ingredients on a serving platter and let sit until they come to room temperature. Just before serving, drizzle the vegetables with the balsamic vinegar. Serve.

tiropitakia

This one comes by way of my Greek heritage. I've never known anyone who could eat just one of these little cheese filo triangles. They may seem a bit complicated to make, but if you want to impress someone, this really works!

½ package filo pastry
½ lb. (225 g) unsalted butter
½ lb. (225 g) ricotta cheese
½ lb. (225 g) feta cheese, crumbled
1 egg
1 tsp. (5 mL) salt
1 tsp. (5 mL) ground black pepper
1 tsp. (5 mL) dried oregano

If the filo is frozen, thaw it in the fridge overnight. Unwrap the filo pastry and cut it in half lengthwise. Return half to the box and store in the freezer for next time.

Cut the filo you will be using into 3-inch-wide (7.5-cm) strips, laying each new section on top of the original one. You'll end up with about 3 sections. Place them on a piece of wax paper, folding the wax paper over to cover the top as well. Next, cover the whole thing with a damp tea towel or cloth. This is most important. The filo is very thin and dries quickly, making it impossible to work with once it dries out. Melt the butter in a saucepan over low heat and keep warm.

Combine the ricotta and feta cheese, egg, salt, pepper and oregano in a medium bowl. Mix to incorporate all the ingredients.

Preheat the oven to 325°F (165°C).

To prepare the triangles, place one strip of filo on your work surface. (Remember to re-cover the filo with the damp cloth as you remove each strip!) Using a pastry brush, brush the filo lightly with melted butter. Place a second filo strip on top of the first and brush it lightly with butter.

Place a tablespoon (15 mL) of the cheese mixture on the bottom of the filo strip, about 2 inches (5 cm) up from the edge. Fold one bottom corner of the filo strip up and over the cheese mixture. This will form a triangle at the bottom of the strip. Fold the point of the triangle up. The bottom edge will now be straight across. (See the diagram.) Continue folding up and across until you reach the end of the strip. You may need to dab a little bit of butter on the edge just before making the final fold, in order to secure it. Continue with the remaining filo and cheese mixture. You will have approximately 30 triangles.

making filo triangles

Preheat the oven to 325°F (165°C). Brush the triangles on both sides with the remaining melted butter and place them on the baking tray. Bake for 10 minutes or until they are golden brown.

You may not want to bake all of these delicious triangles at once. The great thing is you can freeze what you don't want to use immediately. Place the triangles, in a single layer, on a baking sheet and place in the freezer until frozen solid. Transfer them to an airtight container and keep them in the freezer for up to 3 months. Before baking, you may want to brush them lightly on both sides with some melted butter. Bake, from frozen, as above.

spanakopita

This spinach and cheese pie is another recipe of Greek origin. It makes a great start to a dinner or you could cut it into four large pieces and make a meal of it for four people. If you're not a huge fan of spinach you can reduce the amount to half. The spinach/cheese filling can also be used to make filo triangles (page 23), but the filling makes approximately double the number of triangles. If the filo pastry is frozen, thaw it in the fridge overnight, and if it should break or tear while you're preparing the pie, just overlap pieces that fit so you're still creating a layer of filo.

1 lb. (455 g) spinach
$3/_4$ cup (180 mL) unsalted butter
$1/_2$ package frozen filo pastry, thawed
$1/_2$ lb. (225 g) ricotta cheese
$1/_2$ lb. (225 g) feta cheese, crumbled
2 eggs
1 tsp. (5mL) freshly ground black pepper
1 tsp. (5mL) dried oregano
pinch ground nutmeg

Wash the spinach, discarding the big, thick stems, and coarsely chop. Add enough water to a large pot to cook the spinach and place on medium-high heat. When the water comes to a boil, add the spinach and cook for 4 to 5 minutes. Remove the pot from the heat and drain the spinach in a colander. Set aside.

Melt the butter in a saucepan over low heat. While it is melting, prepare the filo pastry. Unwrap the filo and cut it in half widthwise. Return half to the box and store in the freezer for next time. Place the filo between sheets of wax paper and cover with a damp cloth.

Mix the remaining ingredients in a medium bowl until evenly incorporated. When the spinach is cool enough to handle, lightly squeeze it to remove any remaining liquid. Add the spinach to the cheese mixture, mixing it in thoroughly.

Preheat the oven to 350°F (175°C).

Using a pastry brush, brush the baking dish with butter. Lay one sheet of filo in the dish. Using a pastry brush, brush the filo lightly with butter, covering the entire sheet. Repeat, brushing each sheet with butter, until you have 8 sheets of filo layered in the dish. Add the spinach and cheese mixture, smoothing it across the filo but leaving about $1/2$ inch (1.2 cm) around the edges. Top with the remaining sheets of filo, brushing each one with melted butter and allowing them to creep up the edges of the dish. To finish, cut off the edges of the filo that lay over the outside of the pan, but don't cut the edges too close because the filo will shrink when baking.

The next step is optional (my Mom always baked her pie whole). Cut 6 sections just through part of the top layer of filo. Don't cut all the way through or the mixture will leak out and burn the bottom of the pie while baking. Bake for 35 minutes, or until the pie is golden brown. Let stand for 5 minutes before cutting.

basic toaster oven pizza
with variations

SERVES 2

These small pizzas are so easy and absolutely delicious. When it comes to the toppings, let your imagination be your guide. I've provided a few of my favorite variations to get you started.

2 8-inch white flour or whole-wheat tortillas
2 Tbsp. (30 mL) Maria's Roasted Tomato Sauce (page 75)
2 Tbsp. (30 mL) chopped basil
1/2 cup (120 mL) grated mozzarella cheese
2 slices prosciutto (optional)

Preheat the oven to 400°F (200°C).

Toast the tortillas one at a time for about 1 minute. Spoon half the tomato sauce over one tortilla. Sprinkle with half the chopped basil and cheese. Place the slotted tray in the baking dish and place the pizza on the tray. Bake until the cheese is melted and the edges of the tortilla are golden brown, about 5 minutes. If desired, tear one slice of prosciutto into thin strips and place on top of the pizza. Repeat for the second pizza.

roasted veggie pizza:
Omit the prosciutto and mozzarella cheese and substitute 2 Tbsp. (30 mL) chopped olives, 2 slices of roasted red or yellow pepper (see page 61), 2 slices of roasted eggplant (see page 62) and 1 1/2 cup (120 mL) of grated Parmesan cheese.

bbq chicken pizza:

Add 2 Tbsp. (30 mL) barbecue sauce to the tomato sauce. Omit the basil, mozzarella and prosciutto, substituting ½ cup chopped cooked chicken, 2 tsp. (10 mL) finely chopped cilantro, ¼ of a small red onion, thinly sliced, and ½ cup (120 mL) grated Monterey Jack or cheddar cheese. Finish with freshly cracked black pepper.

pesto, sun-dried tomato and goat cheese pizza:

Substitute basil pesto for the tomato sauce. Place ¼ cup (60 mL) of julienned sun-dried tomatoes over top. Replace the mozzarella with ½ cup (120 mL) of crumbled goat cheese. After baking, finish with freshly ground black pepper.

pita crisps

Bake these little "crackers" with whatever spice combinations you like. They go especially well with a hummus dip, or substitute them for ordinary crackers when you're serving soup.

1 Tbsp. (15 mL) dried oregano
1 Tbsp. (15 mL) chili powder
1 Tbsp. (15 mL) ground cumin
$\frac{1}{4}$ cup (60 mL) non-fat sour cream
1 Tbsp. (15 mL) olive oil
2 8-inch (20-cm) pita breads
pinch of salt and freshly ground black pepper

Preheat the oven to 350°F (175°C). Coat the baking dish with olive oil.

Mix the oregano, chili powder, cumin and sour cream in a small bowl. Let stand for 5 minutes.

Split each pita at the sides to form two circles. Brush one side of each pita circle with the sour cream mixture. Cut the circles into 6 wedges.

Place the wedges on the baking dish, coated side up, and bake for 15 minutes, or until the wedges are golden brown and crisp.

Serve warm or cold. Leftovers will keep in an airtight container for 2 weeks.

toasted tomato bread

*This simple appetizer comes by way of Spain. The fresh
tomato rub gives this "toast" a wonderful change of pace.
It pairs well with a cold meat and cheese platter, soup
or salad.*

2 white bread rolls
1 clove garlic
2 small ripe tomatoes
1 Tbsp. (15 mL) extra virgin olive oil
salt and freshly ground black pepper to taste

Split the rolls in half and toast them in the oven. Rub each
slice with the garlic clove, allowing the garlic to "melt"
into the bread. Slice the tomatoes in half and rub the cut
side of the tomato into the toasted rolls, squashing the
flesh and seeds of the tomatoes into the bread. Place the
bread on a serving plate and drizzle with olive oil. Season
with salt and pepper and serve.

mediterranean chicken livers

SERVES 2

Not everyone loves organ meat, but those who do will appreciate my Mom's Mediterranean version of this dish. Velvety and zesty, it will leave you begging for more!

8 chicken livers
1/4 cup (60 mL) olive oil
1/4 cup (60 mL) lemon juice
1/4 cup (60 mL) red wine
1 Tbsp. (15 mL) dried oregano
salt and freshly ground black pepper
2 slices fresh lemon
4 slices baguette

Rinse the chicken livers under cold water and dry them well. In a medium bowl combine the chicken livers with the olive oil, lemon juice, wine, oregano, salt and pepper. Cover the bowl with plastic wrap and place in the fridge. Allow the livers to marinate for at least 1 hour; overnight is even better.

Place the oven rack on the upper setting. Preheat the toaster oven to broil. Place the chicken livers and the marinade in the baking dish and broil for 4 minutes. Remove the baking dish and stir the contents to turn the livers and scrape up bits from the bottom of the dish. Return to the oven and broil for 3 minutes more. Remove and serve on a small platter, garnished with lemon slices and bread to mop up the delicious juices.

spiced nut mix

OK, so you're not at some fancy cocktail lounge eyeing the crowd, but these little cocktail snacks, along with a nice nip of Scotch or glass of Merlot, will have you wondering why anyone would leave the comforts of home.

MAKES
ABOUT 3 CUPS
(720 ML)

4 oz. (113 g) whole unblanched almonds
4 oz. (113 g) walnut pieces
4 oz. (113 g) salted peanuts
1 Tbsp. (15 mL) olive oil
1 tsp. (5 mL) salt
1 tsp. (5 mL) freshly ground black pepper
1 tsp. (5 mL) cayenne pepper
1 tsp. (5 mL) garlic powder
1 tsp. (5 mL) granulated sugar
4 oz. (113 g) plain Cheerios
1 handful pretzel sticks (optional)

Preheat the oven to 350°F (175°C).

Place the nuts in a small bowl and add the olive oil. Stir to coat the nuts in the oil. Add the salt, pepper, cayenne pepper, garlic powder and sugar. Stir to coat the nuts with the spice mixture. Add the Cheerios and toss again.

Place the mixture in the baking dish and spread it out. Bake for 8 to 10 minutes.

Remove and let cool slightly, about 5 minutes. Add the pretzel sticks, if you wish, and toss. Cool completely and serve in a small bowl with your favorite beverage.

Store any leftovers in an airtight container. It will keep for about 1 week.

'shroomin good

SERVES 4

Tiny bites of mushroom stuffed with seasoned crabmeat yield a taste sensation that will surely make your digs the coolest spot in town. I've included a breadcrumb stuffing variation for the vegetarians in the crowd.

16 medium-sized button mushrooms, stems removed
   and chopped
4 Tbsp. (60 mL) olive oil
1 small shallot, minced
¼ cup (60 mL) finely chopped celery
1 Tbsp. (15 mL) dried oregano
¼ cup (60 mL) breadcrumbs
1 Tbsp. (15 mL) chopped fresh parsley
¼ cup (60 mL) finely chopped red bell pepper
½ cup (120 mL) crabmeat (canned is fine, but make
   sure it's well drained)
2 Tbsp. (30 mL) dry vermouth
1 Tbsp. (15 mL) good mayonnaise
1 tsp. (5 mL) lemon juice
¼ tsp. (1.2 mL) dry mustard
pinch of salt and freshly ground black pepper
½ cup (120 mL) grated Parmesan cheese

Preheat the toaster oven to 375°F (190°C).

   Toss the mushroom caps in 2 Tbsp. (30 mL) of the olive oil. Set aside.

Heat the remaining 2 Tbsp. (30 mL) olive oil in a sauté pan over medium heat. Add the mushroom stems, shallot and celery and sauté for 2 minutes. Add the oregano, breadcrumbs, parsley, red pepper, crabmeat and vermouth and sauté for 2 more minutes. Remove from the heat and let cool slightly, about 4 to 5 minutes.

Transfer the mixture to a bowl and add the mayonnaise, lemon juice, mustard, salt, pepper and half the cheese. Mix well. Fill each mushroom cap with the mixture and place on the baking dish. Sprinkle with the remaining Parmesan cheese and bake for 8 minutes, or until the tops are bubbling and golden brown. Serve immediately.

vegetarian stuffing:

Sauté 1 clove of minced garlic with the mushroom stems, shallot and celery. Add 2 Tbsp. (30 mL) of chopped fresh basil to the breadcrumb mixture and substitute an extra $\frac{1}{2}$ cup (120 mL) of breadcrumbs for the crabmeat.

toasted goat cheese

SERVES 2

Serve this with some crisp flatbread crackers, or place it on top of a simple salad of tossed greens, sliced strawberries and a raspberry vinaigrette. It will serve 2, but it all depends on how hungry you are!

1 egg white
4 oz. (113 g) ground almonds (or any combination
    of nuts)
4 oz. (113 g) breadcrumbs
pinch of salt and freshly ground black pepper
1 tsp. (5 mL) mixed dried herbs (thyme, oregano,
    basil, etc.)
1 goat cheese round, about 1 inch thick (2.5 cm) and
    3 inches (7.5 cm) across
1 tsp. (5 mL) olive oil

Preheat the toaster oven to 350°F (175°C).

Beat the egg white in a small bowl. Combine the nuts, breadcrumbs, salt, pepper and dried herbs in another bowl. Dip the goat cheese round into the egg white. Transfer to the dry mixture and coat it completely.

Place the slotted tray in the baking dish and coat the tray with olive oil. Place the cheese on the tray and bake for 15 minutes, or until the crust turns golden brown. Watch carefully, as you don't want the coating to burn. Serve immediately.

roasted red balsamic beets

These add flavor and color to a fresh green salad. Or serve them as an appetizer with a little goat cheese sprinkled on top.

½ cup (120 mL) balsamic vinegar
¼ cup (60 mL) olive oil
salt and freshly ground black pepper to taste
1 Tbsp. (15 mL) dried oregano
1 Tbsp. (15 mL) dried Italian spice mix
4 small beets (about 1 lb./455 g), washed, peeled
   and cut into 16 slices

Preheat the oven to 350°F (175°C).

Combine all the ingredients in a small bowl. Mix well to coat the beets with the marinade. Place in the baking dish, arranging the beets in an even layer. Cover the dish with foil and place in the oven.

After 20 minutes, baste the beets and turn them over. Replace the foil and bake for another 20 minutes. Check and baste again, adding a little more olive oil if the pan is too dry. Bake for another 10 to 20 minutes, or until done. The beets should be tender when pierced with the tip of a knife. Let cool.

Store the beets and their sauce in a non-porous covered dish, as the beet juice can stain. They will keep in the fridge for 1 week.

fennel and goat cheese salad

Fennel has a wonderful, mild, licorice flavor that is mellowed even more by roasting. It pairs perfectly with the goat cheese. This is an easy and elegant salad to begin any meal.

1 medium fennel bulb
2 Tbsp. (30 mL) olive oil
1 Tbsp. (15 mL) balsamic vinegar
1 bunch arugula or watercress
4 oz. (113 g) goat cheese, sliced into 4 equal pieces
coarsely ground black pepper to taste
1 tsp. (5 mL) fresh rosemary leaves
1 cup (240 mL) tear drop or cherry tomatoes

Place the oven rack at the highest setting. Preheat the oven on broil.

Remove the tough or brown outer leaves from the fennel bulb. Trim the bottom and cut off the feathery tops. Cut the bulb into 4 thick slices and place on the baking dish. Brush the fennel with 1 Tbsp. (15 mL) of the olive oil. Broil for 5 minutes, or until nearly tender. Let cool.

Mix the vinegar with the remaining 1 Tbsp. (15 mL) olive oil and set aside.

Arrange the arugula or watercress on a platter or on 4 individual salad plates. Arrange the cheese over the fennel and sprinkle with pepper and rosemary. Just before serving, place the fennel under the hot broiler and cook for about 5 more minutes, or until the cheese has softened. Arrange the fennel on top of the greens. Garnish with tomatoes and drizzle with the oil and vinegar mixture.

parmesan baskets

These baskets are so elegant but undeniably simple! You can serve anything inside them, from a small tossed green salad to pieces of roasted vegetables. The fun part is eating the "dish"!

8 oz. (225 g) Parmesan cheese, coarsely grated

Preheat the oven to 400°F (200°C). Grease the baking dish.

Spread half the cheese into 2 rounds on the dish, making sure the cheese in each round doesn't overlap and the thickness is even. Bake for 8 to 10 minutes, or until the cheese has melted and is golden brown; test by lifting one side with a spatula. Remove and immediately place each round over an inverted drinking glass, shaping the cheese into a basket. Repeat with the remaining cheese. Allow the baskets to cool and harden. Remove from the glasses and store in an airtight container until needed.

parmesan pepper crackers:

These have a real kick to them! Add about 1 tsp. (5 mL) of freshly cracked pepper to each cheese round before baking. After baking, remove them to a large baking sheet covered with wax paper to cool and harden. These make a great garnish for soup or for tomato and onion salad.

baked crab and brie dip

SERVES 8

Try serving this when you've got some new friends coming over. Warm seafood dips and spreads always seem to garner the most compliments—getting your guests talking and mingling. Serve with crackers or toasted slices of French bread and a lovely, crisp Chablis or Fumé Blanc.

8 oz. (225 g) Brie
8 oz. (225 g) cream cheese at room temperature
1 Tbsp. (15 mL) olive oil
1 Tbsp. (15 mL) minced garlic
4 green onions, finely chopped
1 cup (240 mL) half-and-half
1 lb. (455 g) crabmeat
10 oz. (285 g) frozen chopped spinach, thawed and
   squeezed dry
1 6-oz. (170 g) jar marinated artichoke hearts, drained
   and coarsely chopped
1 Tbsp. (15 mL) grainy mustard
1 Tbsp. (15 mL) lemon juice
1 tsp. (5 mL) salt
1 tsp. (5 mL) freshly ground black pepper
1 tsp. (5 mL) dried thyme

Preheat the toaster oven to 425°F (220°C).

Remove the rind from the Brie and discard. Cut the cheese into ½-inch (1.2-cm) pieces. Cut the cream cheese into cubes. Set aside.

Heat the oil in a large sauté pan over medium heat. Add the garlic and onions and sauté for about 3 minutes, until the onion is translucent. Add the Brie and begin to stir. After 1 minute add the cream cheese and half-and-half. Continue to stir until the cheese melts. Remove from the heat.

Pick through the crab to remove any pieces of shell. Add the crab, spinach, artichoke hearts, mustard, lemon juice, salt, pepper and thyme to the sauté pan. Stir gently to mix, then spoon into a greased 2-quart (2-L) casserole dish. Place in the toaster oven and bake for 15 to 20 minutes, or until lightly browned. Serve immediately.

crab-stuffed portobellos

Serves 8

Getting out the hand blender means a little more work, but this dish is well worth it, especially if you're making it for a special occasion. Using fat-free cream cheese and light mayonnaise reduces some of the fat, but I make this at Christmas when there's nothing too rich for my diet. After all, I've been good all year, haven't I? If you can't squeeze all 8 mushroom caps into your dish, bake them in batches.

8 small portobello mushrooms, about 3 to 4 inches
    (7.5 cm to 10 cm) across
8 oz. (225 g) fat-free cream cheese, softened
1/2 cup (120 mL) finely chopped green onions
1/4 cup (60 mL) light mayonnaise
1 tsp. (5 mL) lemon juice
1/2 tsp. (2.5 mL) Spike seasoning
dash of ground red pepper
1 lb. (455 g) crabmeat, shell pieces removed
1 cup (240 mL) quartered cherry tomatoes (about 12)
1/2 cup (120 mL) shredded Swiss cheese
1/2 cup (120 mL) dry breadcrumbs

Preheat the toaster oven to 425°F (220°C).

Remove the brown gills from the undersides of the mushrooms using a spoon. Discard the gills. Remove and discard the stems. Set the mushroom caps aside.

Beat the cream cheese with a hand blender at medium speed until smooth (or beat the cheese by hand with a wooden spoon). Add the green onions, mayonnaise, lemon juice, Spike seasoning and red pepper. Beat well. Stir in the crabmeat, tomatoes and Swiss cheese.

Spoon the mixture evenly into the mushroom caps. Sprinkle each cap with 1 Tbsp. (15 mL) of breadcrumbs. Place in the baking dish and bake for 15 minutes, or until the tops are lightly browned.

notes

brunch

"great for when you've got company"

"a special treat I absolutely adore
with my morning coffee"

"breakfast is ready!"

"warm and savory"

baked eggs

Add bacon, vegetables or cheese to vary this basic recipe. If you or your companion like spice, add chopped jalapeño peppers or hot sauce. Leftover cooked vegetables or meat are also good additions.

soft butter
salt and freshly ground black pepper to taste
2 eggs
2 tsp. (10 mL) half-and-half
1 tsp. (5 mL) melted butter

Preheat the toaster oven to 350°F (175°C). Butter two 4-oz. (113-g) ramekins.

Salt and pepper the two ramekins. Crack 1 egg into each ramekin and drizzle the cream and butter over each.

Transfer the ramekins to the baking dish, placing them so they do not touch the side. Pull out the rack and place the baking dish on it. Pour hot water into the baking dish so it comes halfway up the sides of the ramekins. Bake for 15 minutes, or until the egg yolks are just thickened and the whites are firm. Serve immediately with toast.

baked eggs with roasted vegetables:

Add about 1 Tbsp. (15 mL) of chopped roasted vegetables of your choice and 1 tsp. (5 mL) dried oregano to the bottom of the prepared ramekins. Substitute olive oil for the melted butter and sprinkle with 1 Tbsp. (15 mL) grated Parmesan cheese. When done, serve with 1 Tbsp. (15 mL) of tomato sauce over top.

baked eggs with bacon:

Lightly cook 2 slices of bacon and slice them into 1-inch (2.5-cm) pieces. Place in the bottom of the prepared ramekins. Add the egg, cream and butter and sprinkle the top with some paprika. Serve with thick slices of buttered fresh bread.

breakfast casserole

This lovely layered dish is great for when you've got company. Prepare it the night before so all that's needed is to pop it into the toaster oven while you share coffee and juice with your guests. It's like French toast, but it's from the oven!

2 large eggs
1 cup (240 mL) partly skimmed milk
1 tsp. (5 mL) ground cinnamon
2 Tbsp. (30 mL) maple syrup
10 slices raisin bread, crusts removed
4 oz. (113 g) cream cheese
2 cups (475 mL) diced fresh fruit of your choice

Butter a 2-quart (2-L) casserole dish. Combine the eggs, milk, cinnamon and maple syrup in a large bowl. Slice the bread into triangles. Cover the bottom of the dish with a layer of the bread slices. Top with half the cream cheese. Repeat with another layer of bread and cheese. Cover with the remaining bread.

Pour the egg mixture over the top of the casserole. Cover and refrigerate for at least 2 hours (overnight is best).

Preheat the oven to 350°F (175°C). Bake uncovered for 45 minutes, or until the top is golden brown. Serve with fresh fruit.

ABOVE: tiropitakia (page 23)

PREVIOUS PAGE: basic bruschetta with pesto
(page 16), pesto gorgonzola bruschetta (page 19),
olive walnut bruschetta (page 20)

ABOVE: roasted red balsamic beets (page 37)
FOLLOWING PAGE: goat cheese and chutney
stuffed chicken breasts (page 86)

ABOVE: it's all greek to me leg of lamb (page 116)

PREVIOUS PAGE: asiago potatoes (page 58)

ABOVE: sunday roast chicken (page 80)
FOLLOWING PAGE: lemon poppy seed bread (page 49)

lemon poppy seed bread

A special treat I absolutely adore with my morning coffee. If you don't have an electric or manual hand mixer, you can use a blender.

1 cup (240 mL) sugar
1/3 cup (80 mL) butter, softened
1/2 tsp. (5 mL) lemon juice
3 large egg whites
8 oz. (225 g) carton lemon yogurt
1 2/3 cups (400 mL) all-purpose flour
1/2 cup (120 mL) oat bran
1 tsp. (5 mL) lemon zest
1/2 tsp. (5 mL) baking soda
1/4 tsp. (5 mL) salt
1/4 cup (60 mL) poppy seeds

Preheat the oven to 350°F (175°C). Coat an 8- x 4- x 2-inch (20- x 10- x 5-cm) loaf pan with non-stick spray.

Using a mixer, beat the sugar and butter at medium speed until light and fluffy. Add the lemon juice and egg whites and beat well. Add the yogurt and beat well.

Combine the flour, poppy seeds, oat bran, lemon zest, baking soda and salt in a small bowl. Gradually add the flour mixture to the sugar mixture, stirring just until moist.

Transfer the cake batter into the loaf pan. Bake for 1 hour, or until a toothpick inserted in the center comes out clean. Cool in the pan for 10 minutes on a wire rack; remove from the pan and cool completely.

quick breakfast biscuits

Serve these warm from the toaster oven. They smell incredible! I love spreading them with some softened cream cheese and my favorite fruit preserves. If you don't have self-rising flour, you can use all-purpose flour with 1 1/2 tsp. (7.5 mL) baking powder and an extra 1/2 tsp. (2.5 mL) salt.

1 cup (240 mL) self-rising flour
1 tsp. (5 mL) salt
1 tsp. granulated sugar
1/2 cup (120 mL) milk
2 Tbsp. (30 mL) sour cream

Preheat the toaster oven to 450°F (230°C). Grease a 6-cup muffin pan.

Stir all the ingredients together. Make sure to blend well, but do not overmix. Spoon into the muffin pan. Bake for 12 minutes, or until golden brown. Serve warm.

onion brunch squares

These warm, savory squares make a delicious addition to brunch, but they could easily do duty at the lunch table.

2 Tbsp. (30 mL) butter
2 large onions, finely chopped
1 Tbsp. (15 mL) all-purpose flour
$1/2$ cup (120 mL) sour cream
$1/2$ tsp. (2.5 mL) salt
$1/2$ tsp. (2.5 mL) caraway seeds (optional)
3 eggs, lightly beaten
3 bacon strips, cooked and crumbled
1 8-oz. (225-g) tube refrigerated crescent rolls

Preheat the oven to 375°F (190°C).

Melt the butter in a skillet over medium heat. Add the onions and sauté until tender, about 4 minutes. Cool.

In a medium bowl, blend the flour, sour cream, salt, and caraway seeds, if desired. Add the eggs and mix well. Stir in the bacon and reserved onions.

Unroll the crescent roll dough into the ungreased toaster oven baking dish. Press the seams together to seal. Press the dough 1-inch (2.5 cm) up the sides of the pan. Pour the onion mixture onto the crust. Bake for 25 to 30 minutes, or until a knife inserted near the center comes out clean.

breakfast lasagna

This is perfect for a holiday brunch—layering the ingredients really makes the colors stand out. Serve this with some thick-sliced toast and hot coffee. Breakfast is ready!

3 cups (720 mL) frozen hash browns
3 green onions, chopped
1 yellow bell pepper, chopped
1 red bell pepper, chopped
1 cup (240 mL) button mushrooms, sliced
1 lb. (454 g) bacon, lightly cooked
5 eggs
1/2 cup (120 mL) milk
1 tsp. (5 mL) Italian spice mix
salt and ground black pepper to taste
2 cups (480 mL) grated sharp Cheddar cheese

Preheat the oven to 350°F (175°C).

Place the frozen hash browns in a layer in the bottom of the baking dish. Layer the onion and yellow and red peppers over the hash browns. Layer the mushroom slices on top. Finish with a layer of bacon.

Beat the eggs with the milk and add the Italian spice mix, salt and pepper. Pour the egg mixture over the bacon.

Spread the grated cheese on top. Bake for 35 minutes. Let stand 5 minutes before cutting.

notes

notes

vegetables

"defies imagination"

"rediscover how good real food is"

"the slow roasting brings out
an intense flavor"

"sinfully good taste"

potatoes opa!

Isn't it wonderful when you can return to simple ingredients and rediscover how good real food is? This roasted potato recipe is handed down through every Greek family and it's no surprise that the rest of the world loves it too! You could add carrots to this recipe and make a bigger side dish. Opa, my friend!

4 medium potatoes
½ cup (120 mL) olive oil
1 tsp. (5 mL) salt
1 tsp. (5 mL) freshly ground black pepper
1 Tbsp. (15 mL) dried oregano
1 tsp. (5 mL) garlic powder or 1 minced clove garlic
½ lemon

Preheat the oven to 400°F (200°C).

Peel the potatoes and cut them into 1-inch-thick (2.5-cm) slices. In a bowl, combine the potatoes, olive oil, salt, pepper, oregano and garlic. Toss well and transfer to the baking dish. Squeeze the lemon over the potatoes. Bake for 15 minutes, then reduce the heat to 350°F (175°C). Continue baking for another 20 minutes, occasionally removing the pan to toss. Potatoes are done when they're golden brown, slightly crispy, yet tender when poked with a fork.

sweet potato pie

So easy it almost defies the imagination. This is great as a side dish for ham or a light main course with a salad.

1¹/₂ lbs. (680 g) sweet potatoes
¹/₄ cup (60 mL) sour cream
¹/₄ cup (60 mL) heavy cream
2 whole eggs
2 egg yolks
2 Tbsp. (30 mL) chopped fresh sage
1 tsp. (5 mL) ground nutmeg
1 Tbsp. (15 mL) lime juice
1 tsp. (5 mL) ground cumin
1 Tbsp. (15 mL) maple syrup
¹/₂ tsp. (2.5 mL) salt
freshly ground black pepper to taste
1 frozen prebaked pie crust (8 or 9 inches/20 or 23 cm),
    thawed

Boil the potatoes whole, in a large saucepan of water, until they are tender. Drain and rinse under cold water until they are easy to handle. Peel and place in a medium bowl.

Preheat the toaster oven to 400°F (200°C).

Add the sour cream and heavy cream to the sweet potatoes and mash until smooth. Stir in the eggs and egg yolks, sage, nutmeg, lime juice, cumin, maple syrup, salt and pepper.

Pour into the pie shell, smooth the top and bake for 35 minutes. The crust should be golden brown and the center of the pie set. When a toothpick inserted into the center comes out clean, it's done. Allow the pie to sit for 10 minutes before cutting.

asiago potatoes

This recipe has been adapted from the standard scalloped potatoes with the addition of Asiago cheese. You can parboil the potatoes first to reduce the cooking time by half.

1½ tsp. (7.5 mL) butter
4 peeled Yukon Gold potatoes, peeled and sliced
    about ¼ inch (.5 cm) thick
2 green onions, sliced into ¼-inch (.5-cm) pieces
2 oz. (125 g) Asiago cheese, coarsely grated
¼ tsp. (2 mL) ground nutmeg
½ tsp. (2.5 mL) salt
½ cup (120 mL) whole milk
1 cup (240 mL) half-and-half
¼ tsp. (1.2 mL) paprika

Preheat the oven to 325°F (165°C). Generously butter a 2-quart (2-L) casserole dish.

Place the potatoes, onions and cheese in a large mixing bowl. Sprinkle with the nutmeg and salt and mix well to combine all the ingredients. Place in the casserole dish, pressing the potatoes down to form an even layer. Mix the milk and cream together and pour over the potatoes. Press the potatoes down again, into the cream mixture. Sprinkle the top with paprika.

Cover the top of the dish loosely with foil. Bake for 45 minutes, then remove the foil and baste with the cream mixture. Bake, uncovered, for 20 minutes longer.

Baste with the cream mixture once again and continue to bake uncovered for 15 to 20 minutes more, until the potatoes are very tender and the top is golden brown. Let stand 10 minutes before cutting and serving.

irie potatoes

This adaptation of the classic Greek potato recipe makes use of the natural sugar in sweet potatoes and combines it with the tang of freshly squeezed lime juice. I love to serve this with fish. No problem, Mon!

1 medium sweet potato, peeled
½ cup (120 mL) olive oil
1 tsp. (5 mL) salt
1 tsp. (5 mL) freshly ground black pepper
1 Tbsp. (15 mL) allspice powder
1 Tbsp. (15 mL) ground cinnamon
1 Tbsp. (15 mL) ground coriander
1 tsp. (5 mL) garlic powder or 1 minced clove garlic
1 lime

Preheat the oven to 400°F (200°C).

Cut the sweet potato into ½-inch-thick (1.2-cm) slices. In a bowl, combine the sweet potato with the olive oil, salt, pepper, allspice, cinnamon, coriander and garlic. Toss to combine and transfer to the baking pan. Squeeze lime juice over the potatoes. Bake for 15 minutes, then reduce the heat to 350°F (175°C). Continue baking for another 20 minutes, occasionally removing the pan to turn the potatoes. The potatoes are done when they're golden brown, slightly crispy, yet tender when tested with a fork.

roasted tomatoes

MAKES ¹/₂ TO
1 CUP (120 TO
240 ML)

These tomatoes make a wonderful addition to pasta, bruschetta or a sandwich. The slow roasting brings out an intense flavor and caramelizes the natural sugars present in tomatoes.

3 Roma tomatoes
olive oil
salt and freshly ground black pepper to taste

Preheat the oven to 300°F (150°C).

Slice the tomatoes ¹/₄ inch (.6 cm) thick and place them in a bowl. Drizzle with olive oil and add the salt and pepper. Toss to coat the tomatoes.

Insert the slotted tray into the baking dish. Lay the tomato slices on the tray, spacing them evenly. Bake for 40 minutes, turning once halfway through cooking. The tomatoes are done when they are slightly dry without being burnt. They should have a rich red color, almost like a sun-dried tomato.

Let cool and refrigerate in an airtight container. They will keep for about 1 week.

roasted peppers

Intense color and sinfully good taste—roasted peppers are an integral part of a number of recipes in this book.

MAKES ¹/₂ TO 1 CUP (120 TO 240 ML)

2 red bell peppers (or a combination of colors)
olive oil
1 Tbsp. (15 mL) balsamic vinegar

Preheat the oven on broil.

Cut the peppers in half and remove the seeds and membranes. Place them in a bowl and drizzle with olive oil.

Place the slotted tray in the baking dish. Lay the peppers skin side up on the slotted tray. Broil until the skins become blackened, about 15 to 20 minutes.

Remove the peppers from the oven and place them in a paper bag. Close the bag and let the peppers sweat for about 15 minutes. Remove them from the bag and peel off the blackened skins. Transfer to an airtight container and drizzle with some more olive oil and the balsamic vinegar. Will keep for 1 week in the refrigerator.

roasted eggplant

Salting the eggplant allows it to excrete some of its bitter juice. Its flavor and meaty texture make it a hearty addition to many recipes.

1 medium eggplant
salt
olive oil
1 Tbsp. (15 mL) balsamic vinegar

Slice the eggplant into ½-inch-thick (1.2-cm) slices. Salt one side of the eggplant slices and lay on a paper towel to drain for about 10 minutes. Repeat on the other side. Wipe each side with a paper towel to remove leftover salt.

Preheat the toaster oven to 325°F (160°C).

Place the eggplant in a bowl and drizzle with olive oil. Toss to coat the eggplant with oil. Lay the eggplant slices on the baking dish. Bake for 15 minutes, or until the skin of the eggplant becomes dry and shrinks a bit. Remove from the oven and let cool.

Transfer to an airtight container and drizzle with some more olive oil and the balsamic vinegar. Will keep for 1 week in the refrigerator.

roasted balsamic onions

This recipe calls for using chipolline onions—small cocktail-like onions usually found in an Italian market—but you could easily substitute pearl onions or 3 small onions cut into 8 pieces each (don't worry if the layers fall apart when using regular onions).

MAKE 1 TO
1 1/2 CUPS
(240 TO
360 ML)

20 chipolline or pearl onions
1/2 cup (120 mL) olive oil
4 Tbsp. (60 mL) balsamic vinegar
salt and freshly ground black pepper to taste

Preheat the oven to 325°F (160°C).

Remove the skins from the onions. In a small bowl, combine the onions, olive oil, 3 Tbsp. (45 mL) of the balsamic vinegar and salt and pepper. Mix together.

Place the onions and their marinade in the baking dish. Cover the dish with foil and bake for 15 minutes.

Remove the foil carefully—watch out for the steam—and continue to roast the onions for 5 more minutes, until they're tender and lightly browned. Remove and let cool. Transfer to an airtight container and drizzle over the remaining 1 Tbsp. (15 mL) of balsamic vinegar. Store in the refrigerator for up to 1 week.

roasted artichoke hearts

Baby artichokes are best, but if they're not in season mature ones will work. The lemon juice is the critical ingredient in this recipe, keeping the artichokes from browning (oxidizing) and giving them a fresh citrus flavor. These are great hot or cold, alone or in another recipe!

2 lemons
10 baby artichokes or 4 large ones
½ cup (120 mL) olive oil
1 tsp. (5 mL) salt
1 tsp. (5 mL) freshly ground black pepper
1 tsp. (5 mL) garlic powder
1 tsp. (5 mL) Italian spice mix

Preheat the oven to 350°F (175°C). Prepare a bowl of cold water by adding the juice of 1 lemon and the squeezed lemon pieces.

Clean the artichokes. This requires minimal trimming for baby artichokes but slightly more work for mature ones. For baby ones, trim the stems a bit and peel away the tougher base leaves on the bottom third of the artichoke. Cut the artichokes in half and check for a choke. Baby artichokes rarely have one. If they do, pluck it out with a knife. For mature artichokes, trim the stems a bit more and peel some of the tough skin off the sides of the stem. Remove about ½ inch (1.2 cm) from the tops of the artichokes. Peel away the bottom leaves from the bottom half of the artichoke. Cut the artichokes in half. Using your knife, carefully cut under and around the choke and remove it. Slice the halves in half again.

Place each artichoke piece into the water/lemon mixture as you work, as they will darken when exposed to the air. Allow the artichokes to soak for 15 minutes.

In another bowl, combine the juice of the remaining lemon, olive oil, salt, pepper, garlic powder and Italian spice mix. Drain the artichokes and pat them dry. Place them in the marinade. Transfer the mixture to the baking dish, placing the artichokes cut side down.

Roast uncovered for 30 minutes. Remove from the oven and cover loosely with a piece of foil. Return to the oven and bake for another 20 to 30 minutes, or until done. They should be moist and soft when pierced with a fork.

Allow them to cool and transfer to an airtight container. They will keep in the refrigerator for 1 week.

roasted zucchini

MAKE 8 TO
10 SLICES

Sweet, succulent zucchini is one of those vegetables that enhance any meal. This recipe is used in Toasted Antipasto (page 22) and in Tomato and Eggplant Pasta Bake (page 128) but it can stand up as a side dish on its own. Depending on the size of the zucchini, you may have to do this in two batches.

1 large or 2 medium zucchini
$1/4$ cup (60 mL) olive oil
2 Tbsp. (30 mL) balsamic vinegar
salt and freshly ground black pepper to taste

Preheat the oven on broil.

Cut the ends off the zucchini and slice the zucchini lengthwise, into $1/4$-inch-thick (.6-cm) slices. Mix the oil, balsamic vinegar, salt and pepper in a small bowl.

Place the slotted tray in the baking dish and lay the zucchini slices out in a single layer. Brush the zucchini with the marinade. Broil for 3 minutes. Remove the dish and turn the zucchini slices over. Brush with the marinade and broil for 3 minutes longer. Let cool and place the zucchini in an airtight container with the rest of the marinade. Store in the refrigerator for up to 1 week.

roasted asparagus

This is so simple to prepare, yet is so delicious. Get the best olive oil you can to flavor these tender vegetables.

1 lb. (455 g) asparagus
1/2 cup (120 mL) extra virgin olive oil or flavored oil
dash salt and freshly ground black pepper to taste

Preheat the oven and the baking dish to 400°F (200°C).

Clean and trim the asparagus. Snap off and discard the tough ends. Toss the asparagus in 1/4 cup (60 mL) of the olive oil.

Place in the baking dish and roast for 10 minutes, turning the asparagus once or twice. Remove from the oven and place the asparagus on a serving tray. Finish with the remaining 1/4 cup (60 mL) olive oil and a sprinkle of salt and pepper. Serve immediately.

sweet roasted squash

SERVES 4 *Roasted squash is such a versatile vegetable, standing up well to all meat and pasta. I like it with roast turkey—it complements my holiday bird each year. When baked in the toaster oven it doesn't have to fight for space with the gigantic bird that roasts in the conventional oven.*

1 medium acorn squash
1 Tbsp. (15 mL) butter
1 tsp. (5 mL) salt
1 tsp. (5 mL) freshly ground black pepper
1 Tbsp. (22.5 mL) brown sugar
1½ tsp. (7.5 mL) brown sugar
fresh parsley leaves, for garnish

Preheat the toaster oven to 350°F (175°C).

Cut the squash in half. If the pieces do not sit flat when placed cut side up, you can slice a small piece off the bottom. Clean out and discard the seeds and membranes.

Butter the cut side and inside of the squash. Use a little extra if you don't have enough butter to cover the whole cut surface and cavity. Distribute the salt, pepper and the 1 Tbsp. (15 mL) brown sugar evenly in the cavities.

Cut two pieces of foil, large enough to enclose each piece of squash. Place a squash half in the center of each piece of foil and fold the foil to seal it on top and at each end. Place in the baking dish and bake for 45 minutes.

Remove the dish and carefully open the foil pouches, but do not remove the squash from them. Peel them back to expose the tops and return the dish to the oven for 15 more minutes.

Let cool slightly and then carefully scrape the squash meat into a bowl. Add the 1½ tsp. (7.5 mL) brown sugar and mix to create a smooth consistency. Garnish with parsley leaves.

green beans sto fourno

Literally, green beans done in the oven. I look forward to this dish when young green beans are in season. Serve with any meat or fish of your choice.

SERVES 2

6 oz. (170 g) green beans
2 medium tomatoes, seeded and chopped
2 Tbsp. (30 mL) olive oil
juice of ½ lemon
2 Tbsp. (30 mL) dried mint
1 Tbsp. (15 mL) dried oregano
salt and freshly ground black pepper to taste

Preheat the toaster oven to 400°F (200°C).

Trim the stem ends of the green beans. Place the beans in boiling water for 2 minutes. Remove the beans, drain them and then plunge them into a bowl of cold water for 2 minutes. Drain again. Place the beans in a bowl with all the other ingredients. Toss to coat.

Place the mixture in the baking dish and bake for 10 minutes. Remove the dish and stir the beans. Return to the oven for 3 minutes. Serve immediately.

yemista (mint stuffed vegetables)

Once again my Greek heritage has provided me with one of the most delicious and light meals around. If you can find zucchini blossoms, go for it, but the standard tomato, eggplant, pepper or zucchini works beautifully. Tomatoes are best stuffed when they're in season, and winter tomatoes may not hold up in the oven. I make extra stuffing so that I can add ground meat to it to make a casserole.

1 medium eggplant

2 medium zucchini

2 medium tomatoes

2 medium bell peppers (yellow, green or red)

2 medium Yukon gold potatoes

1 medium onion, finely chopped

1 cup (240 mL) uncooked long-grain rice

2 Roma tomatoes, coarsely chopped

2 cloves garlic, mashed

$\frac{1}{4}$ cup (60 mL) dried mint ($\frac{1}{2}$ cup, 120 mL fresh)

1 Tbsp. (15 mL) salt

1 Tbsp. (15 mL) freshly ground black pepper

1 Tbsp. (15 mL) dried oregano

3 Tbsp. (45 mL) tomato paste

$\frac{1}{2}$ cup (60 mL) olive oil

$\frac{1}{2}$ cup (60 mL) water

Preheat the oven to 375°F (190°C).

Remove about $\frac{1}{4}$ inch (.6 cm) from the tops of the eggplant and 1 of the zucchini, reserving the ends. Using a long, thin spoon, scoop out the inside of the eggplant and zucchini, leaving about $1/4$ inch (.6 cm) around the sides and $1/2$ inch (1.2 cm) on the bottom. Be careful not to scoop the whole way through. Finely chop the insides and set aside in a large bowl.

Cut the tops off the tomatoes and the bell pepper. Reserve the tops. Scoop out the insides of the tomatoes and add to the reserved eggplant and zucchini mixture. Scoop out and discard the seeds and membranes of the pepper. Place the vegetables into a 2-quart (2-L) casserole dish or the toaster oven baking dish.

Grate the potatoes and the second zucchini with a coarse grater. Add the grated potatoes and zucchini to the bowl with the reserved eggplant, zucchini and tomatoes. Add the onion, rice, chopped Roma tomatoes, garlic, mint, salt, black pepper, oregano, 2 Tbsp. (30 mL) of the tomato paste and $1/4$ cup (60 mL) of the olive oil. Mix well.

Stuff each vegetable with the mixture. Place a reserved end on top of each vegetable. Drizzle the remaining $1/4$ cup (60 mL) of olive oil over the stuffed vegetables. Mix the remaining 1 Tbsp. (15 mL) of tomato paste and water together in a small bowl and pour it into the casserole dish.

Bake uncovered for 45 minutes, occasionally basting the stuffed vegetables with the liquid. Add a little more water if it reduces too quickly. Cover the dish loosely with foil and return to the oven for another 30 minutes. Approximately half of the liquid will have evaporated. Let sit for 10 minutes before serving.

veggies lakonia

SERVES 2

This one's from the family archives. Use real Greek extra virgin olive oil and fresh mint, and you'll swear your kitchen was transported to a quaint Greek village. Serve as a side dish or as a light vegetarian main course, with crusty bread and feta cheese. A nice, crisp, dry white wine would make a great finish to the flavors. Yasoo!

3 medium potatoes, peeled and quartered
2 medium zucchini, cut into 1-inch-thick (2.5-cm) slices
1 medium eggplant, quartered and cut into 1-inch-thick (2.5-cm) pieces
3 celery stalks, chopped into 3-inch-thick (7.5-cm) pieces
$\frac{1}{4}$ cup (60 mL) olive oil
$\frac{1}{2}$ 5-oz. (140-mL) can tomato paste
5 cloves garlic, sliced in half
$\frac{1}{4}$ cup (60 mL) chopped fresh mint or 2 Tbsp. (30 mL) dried mint
1 Tbsp. (15 mL) dried Greek oregano
dash of salt and freshly ground black pepper to taste
1 tomato, roughly chopped
$\frac{1}{2}$ cup (120 mL) water

Preheat the oven to 400°F (200°C).

Combine the potatoes, zucchini, eggplant and celery in a bowl. Add the olive oil, tomato paste, garlic, chopped mint, oregano, salt and pepper. Toss to coat the vegetables evenly and transfer to the baking pan. Distribute the chopped tomato evenly over the vegetable mixture. Pour the water over the vegetables. Bake for 15 minutes. Reduce the heat to 350°F (175°C) and continue cooking for 30 to 40 minutes, or until the potatoes are tender when pierced with a fork.

no crust vegetable pie

A healthy version of a higher-fat quiche, the flour in the fill-ing settles as it bakes, forming a mock crust.

2 tsp. (10 mL) olive oil
2 medium red bell peppers, diced
1 medium green bell pepper, diced
1 medium onion, minced
1 cup chopped tomato
2 whole eggs
3 egg whites
1 cup (240 mL) milk
$^{1}/_{4}$ cup (60 mL) grated Parmesan cheese
$^{1}/_{4}$ tsp. (1.2 mL) salt
$^{1}/_{4}$ tsp. (1.2 mL) black pepper
$^{2}/_{3}$ cup (160 mL) flour
1 cup (240 mL) bottled salsa

Heat the olive oil over low heat in a large non-stick skillet. Add the bell peppers and onion, and cook, stirring fre-quently, until the vegetables have softened, about 5 min-utes. Stir in the tomato and cook until almost all the liquid has evaporated, about 5 minutes. Set aside to cool.

Preheat the oven to 350°F (175°C). Spray the baking dish with vegetable cooking spray.

In a large bowl, whisk together the whole eggs and egg whites. Stir in the milk, Parmesan, salt and black pepper, and mix until well combined. Whisk in the flour.

Transfer the vegetables to the baking dish and pour the egg mixture over the vegetables. Bake until the eggs are just set, about 35 minutes. Cool the pie for 10 minutes before cutting into 6 squares. Serve topped with salsa.

spinach casserole

This can be prepared a day ahead of time and refrigerated. Just add 30 minutes to the baking time.

1/4 cup (60 mL) butter
1/2 cup (120 mL) chopped onions
1 cup (240 mL) sliced shiitake mushrooms
2 10-oz. (284-g) packages frozen chopped spinach, thawed and drained
1 Tbsp. (15 mL) Worcestershire sauce
1 6-oz. (170-g) package cream cheese, at room temperature, cut into cubes
1/2 tsp. (2.5 mL) salt
1/4 tsp. (1.2 mL) freshly ground black pepper
1/4 tsp. (1.2 mL) ground nutmeg

Preheat the oven to 375°F (190°C).

Melt the butter in a saucepan over medium heat. Add the onions and mushrooms and sauté for about 5 minutes. Squeeze the spinach dry using paper towels. Add the spinach, Worcestershire sauce, cream cheese, salt, pepper and nutmeg. Cook until the cream cheese has melted. Spoon into a greased 2-quart (2-L) casserole dish and bake for 15 to 20 minutes. Serve warm.

maria's roasted tomato sauce

I love this sauce not only because it's so easy but because it tastes so good. I use it constantly, in pastas, vegetable dishes, on meats or even as a dip! If you want it spicy, add some hot pepper flakes to the recipe.

MAKES
ABOUT 1 CUP
(240 ML)

6 large field tomatoes
½ cup (120 mL) chopped fresh basil
2 Tbsp. (30 mL) dried oregano
1 tsp. (5 mL) garlic powder
1 Tbsp. (15 mL) salt
1 Tbsp. (15 mL) freshly ground black pepper
1 Tbsp. (15 mL) sugar
½ cup (120 mL) olive oil

Preheat the toaster oven to 350°F (175°C).

Cut the tomatoes into chunks and place in the baking dish. Add the remaining ingredients and toss to coat.

Bake uncovered for 30 minutes. Remove and stir. Return to the oven for another 30 minutes. The tomatoes should not be watery and the sauce should look thick. The sauce will keep in the refrigerator for up to 1 week.

notes

main courses

"it doesn't get much simpler than this"

"savory and delicious!"

"a sweet and sour, sticky delight!"

"satisfy your cravings"

parmesan chicken

Simple, quick and tasty. It doesn't get much easier than this.

2 chicken breast halves
2 Tbsp. (30 mL) olive oil
2 Tbsp. (30 mL) finely ground Parmigiano-Reggiano
     cheese
1 Tbsp. (15 mL) Italian spice mix
1 clove garlic, minced
salt and freshly ground black pepper to taste

Preheat the oven, the slotted pan and the baking dish to 375°F (190°C).

Rinse the chicken and pat it dry. In a medium bowl, mix together the olive oil, cheese, spice mix and garlic. Coat the chicken breasts evenly in the mixture.

Place the chicken on the slotted pan in the baking dish and season with salt and pepper. Bake for 20 minutes and baste with the juices in the bottom of the pan. Bake for another 10 minutes. Pierce the chicken with a fork. It is done when the juices run clear. Serve immediately.

lemon chicken breasts

Chicken and citrus get along famously. If you have a lime you could use that instead of the lemon. The idea here is to let the flavor of the chicken shine through with subtle spicing and the zing of the lemon. This is nice with a rice pilaf.

SERVES 2

2 boneless, skinless chicken breast halves
$^1/_2$ cup (120 mL) olive oil
juice of 1 lemon
1 tsp. (5 mL) salt
1 tsp. (5 mL) freshly ground black pepper
1 tsp. (5 mL) dried oregano

Rinse the chicken and pat it dry. Place the remaining ingredients in a bowl and mix. Coat the chicken in the mixture and, if you have time, marinate the chicken in the fridge for at least 1 hour.

Preheat the oven on broil.

Place the slotted tray in the baking dish. Lay the chicken breasts on the tray and broil for 5 minutes. Remove from the oven and turn the chicken over. Broil for about 10 more minutes, or until the juices run clear when the chicken is pierced with a fork. Serve immediately.

sunday roast chicken

SERVES 2

My toaster oven has a large capacity so I can actually roast a whole bird. I've adapted this to work for any toaster oven by using half a chicken. Just ask your butcher to split the chicken down the backbone and breastbone. Freeze the other half for the next time you make the dish. If you want to try roasting a whole chicken, double the goat cheese, rosemary and lemon used and increase the covered cooking time by 45 minutes.

½ of a 3-lb. (1.4-kg) roasting chicken
2 oz. (57 g) goat cheese, sliced ¼ inch thick
2 sprigs fresh rosemary
½ cup (120 mL) olive oil
1 lemon, cut in half
salt and ground black pepper to taste
1 Tbsp. (15 mL) fresh herbs of your choice

Rinse the chicken and pat it dry. Preheat the oven to 400°F (200°C).

Place the chicken in a bowl. Using your fingertips, carefully lift the skin on the breast and the thigh of the chicken. Place slices of the goat cheese and the fresh rosemary sprigs between the skin and meat. Coat the chicken in olive oil and squeeze the lemon juice over the chicken. Reserve the lemon skins. Sprinkle the salt, pepper and herbs over the chicken.

Cut a large sheet of foil and place the chicken in the center. Place the squeezed lemon skins inside the cavity of the chicken. Pour the marinade remaining in the bowl over the chicken and seal the foil, making a package.

Place the package in the baking dish and bake for 45 minutes. Remove from the oven and carefully cut the foil down the center. Peel the foil back to expose the chicken. Return to the oven for 15 minutes to brown the top of the chicken.

Remove from the oven and allow the chicken to sit for 10 minutes. Transfer to a platter and pour the collected juices over the top. Serve immediately.

horiatiki chicken and rice

SERVES 4

This is what I crave when I go home to my parents' house. I prefer it with chicken legs but you can make it with chicken breasts. The chicken is extra moist with the skin on, but for a lighter version, use skinless chicken cuts. This recipe is rustic, easy to prepare and a full meal all in one pan. Using chicken stock instead of water adds intensity to the flavor!

4 large chicken legs or breasts (bone in)
1 5-oz. (140-mL) can tomato paste
2 cloves garlic, chopped
4 cups (950 mL) hot chicken stock or water
$\frac{1}{4}$ cup (60 mL) melted butter
1 Tbsp. (15 mL) salt
1 tsp. (5 mL) freshly ground black pepper
1 Tbsp. (15 mL) dried oregano
1 cup (240 mL) long-grain rice

Preheat the oven to 350°F (175°C).

Rinse the chicken but do not pat dry. Place the chicken pieces in a large bowl and toss them with the tomato paste. Transfer to the baking dish and distribute the garlic over top. Pour 1½ cups (360 mL) of the hot chicken stock or water into the bowl the chicken was in, to capture any remaining tomato paste, then pour over the chicken. Pour the melted butter over top of the chicken. Bake uncovered for 30 minutes. (If using chicken breasts, cover with foil after 20 minutes.)

Remove the chicken from the pan and place on a dish with a tent of foil to keep it warm. Add the remaining 2½ cups (600 mL) of chicken stock or water to the baking dish. Stir in the salt, pepper, oregano and rice. Return to the oven and bake for 20 minutes. Check the rice at this stage. If it's cooking too fast or seems dry, add a little more chicken stock or water and cover the dish loosely with foil. Continue baking for 10 minutes, or until the rice is done.

Return the chicken to the baking dish and bake for 5 more minutes. Serve immediately.

chicken cacciatore

So easy it gives you extra time to enjoy your guests. Serve this with hot buttered spaghetti or rice. Put your rice or pasta water on about 20 minutes before the chicken is done and you're ready to go.

4 boneless, skinless chicken breast halves
$^1/_2$ cup (120 mL) Maria's Roasted Tomato Sauce
1 red bell pepper, roughly chopped
1 tsp. (5 mL) ground oregano
1 tsp. (5 mL) celery salt
$^1/_4$ cup (60 mL) white wine
1 tsp. (5 mL) garlic salt
$^1/_2$ tsp. (5 mL) black pepper
$^1/_2$ cup (120 mL) canned, crushed tomatoes
$^1/_2$ cup (120 mL) grated Parmigiano-Reggiano cheese
1 Tbsp. (15 mL) chopped parsley

Preheat the oven to 425°F (220°C).

Rinse the chicken and pat it dry. Coat the baking dish with olive oil and place the chicken in the dish. Combine the tomato sauce, bell pepper, oregano, celery salt, wine, garlic salt, pepper and tomatoes in a bowl and pour over the chicken. Cover the baking dish with foil and bake for 1 hour.

Sprinkle with the cheese and parsley before serving.

chicken salsa

SERVES 2

This is one of my honey's favorites. If he's really good, I make extra—this recipe can easily be doubled. Delicious served with rice—if there's any juice left in the pan, pour it over the rice. If you like your chicken really spicy, add chopped jalapeños. Mucho caliente!

2 boneless, skinless chicken breast halves
1 tomato, seeded and chopped
1/2 avocado, chopped
1/4 cup (60 mL) olive oil
2 Tbsp. (30 mL) lime juice
2 Tbsp. (30 mL) chopped fresh cilantro
1 tsp. (5 mL) salt
1 tsp. (5 mL) black pepper
1 tsp. (5 mL) Spike seasoning
dash of hot sauce (optional)

Preheat the oven on broil.

Rinse the chicken breasts and pat them dry. Combine the tomato, avocado, olive oil, lime juice, 1 Tbsp. (15 mL) of the cilantro, salt, pepper, Spike seasoning and hot sauce, if desired, together in a bowl. Add the chicken breasts and marinate for 15 minutes.

Place the slotted tray in the oven baking dish. Remove the chicken breasts from the marinade and place on the slotted tray. Pour the marinade over the chicken. Broil for 15 minutes. The juices should run clear when the chicken is pierced with a fork. Let sit for 1 minute and sprinkle with the remaining 1 Tbsp. (15 mL) of cilantro before serving.

goat cheese and chutney
stuffed chicken breasts

If you want to treat yourself (and maybe someone else) to a really fabulous meal, now is the time! This isn't as complicated as it sounds and makes a great presentation. I like to have it with mashed sweet potatoes.

2 large boneless, skinless chicken breast halves
salt and freshly ground black pepper to taste
2 oz. (57 g) goat cheese
2 Tbsp. (30 mL) peach chutney (or whatever kind
    you prefer)
4 basil leaves
1/4 cup (60 mL) olive oil
juice of 1/2 lemon
1 tsp. (5 mL) Spike seasoning
1 tsp. (5 mL) dried Italian herb mix

Rinse the chicken and pat it dry. Lay the chicken on a cutting board with the inside of the breast facing up. Cover with a sheet of plastic wrap. Using a mallet (or your hammer), carefully whack the chicken to even out the thickness. Be careful not to hit it too hard or you'll break it apart.

Remove the plastic wrap and sprinkle the chicken with salt and pepper. Place half the goat cheese, 1 Tbsp. (15 mL) of the chutney and 2 basil leaves on each chicken breast. Fold the chicken breast over to cover the dressing. Using butcher's string, tie the chicken in three places along each breast.

Preheat the oven to 375°F (190°C). Place the slotted tray in the baking dish.

Cut a piece of foil large enough to enclose both chicken breasts. Place the chicken in the center of the foil and coat with the olive oil, lemon juice, Spike seasoning and Italian herb mix. Fold the foil to seal the package and place it on the slotted tray. Bake for 30 minutes. Remove from the oven and open the foil carefully—watch for steam. Fold the foil back to expose the chicken and return to the oven for 10 to 15 minutes more. Remove from the oven and let rest for 5 minutes before transferring to a platter. Cut the chicken breasts into 1-inch (2.5-cm) slices and spoon the sauce from the foil pouch over the breasts.

A Chuckle A Day...®
from the Medical Comm

moroccan chicken

Serves 2

The raisins and olives in this dish perfume the
the mixture of sweet and savory really gives your
lift. Great with roast potatoes or rice.

2 boneless skinless chicken breast halves
2 Tbsp. (30 mL) butter
½ cup (120 mL) cracked green olives
½ cup (120 mL) raisins
½ cup (120 mL) chopped green onions
2 Tbsp. (30 mL) olive oil
juice of ½ lemon
¼ tsp. (1.2 mL) ground cinnamon
¼ tsp. (1.2 mL) ground coriander
2 cloves garlic, minced
1 tsp. (5 mL) salt
1 tsp. (5 mL) freshly ground black pepper
½ cup (120 mL) chicken stock or water
2 Tbsp. (30 mL) chopped fresh cilantro

Preheat the oven to 350°F (175°C).

Rinse the chicken and pat it dry. Melt the butter in a pan over medium-high heat. When the butter is golden brown (but not burnt), add the chicken and sear both sides, about 2 minutes per side.

Transfer the chicken to the baking dish. Combine all the other ingredients, except the cilantro, in a bowl and pour over the chicken. Bake for 20 minutes, until the juices run clear when the chicken is pierced with a fork. Transfer to a platter and sprinkle with cilantro.

chicken fingers

Sometimes I like to hang out in sweats, watch a movie and eat something that requires fingers only. This recipe serves just that purpose. Serve it with plum sauce, honey mustard or ranch dressing. You can prepare a whole chicken breast the same way, if you want, and serve a proper meal with vegetables. Bake a whole breast for about 35 to 40 minutes.

SERVES 1

1 boneless, skinless chicken breast half, or
    8 chicken tenders
$1/2$ cup (120 mL) sour cream
$1/4$ cup (60 mL) milk
1 Tbsp. (15 mL) Dijon mustard
$1/2$ cup (120 mL) finely grated Parmesan cheese
$1/2$ cup (120 mL) breadcrumbs
1 tsp. (5 mL) garlic powder
1 tsp. (5 mL) dried oregano
1 tsp. (5 mL) ground cumin
1 tsp. (5 mL) salt
1 tsp. (5 mL) freshly ground black pepper

Rinse the chicken and pat it dry. Cut the chicken breast into 1-inch (2.5-cm) strips. Preheat the oven to 350°F (175°C).

In one bowl, combine the sour cream, milk and mustard. In another bowl combine the cheese, breadcrumbs, garlic powder, oregano, cumin, salt and pepper. Coat the chicken strips in the sour cream mixture, then transfer to the breadcrumb mixture and coat the surface. Use your fingers to help the crumbs adhere to the chicken strips. Place the chicken strips in the baking dish and bake until the coating is golden brown, about 30 minutes.

toasted chicken casserole

Try this when you've got leftover chicken. I like asparagus in this dish but you can add any vegetables you wish.

3 Tbsp. (45 mL) butter
1/2 cup (120 mL) chopped button mushrooms
1/4 cup (60 mL) flour
1 cup (240 mL) chicken stock
3/4 cup (180 mL) half-and-half
2 cups (475 mL) chopped cooked chicken
    (bite-sized pieces)
2 Tbsp. (30 mL) lemon juice
2 Tbsp. (30 mL) dry vermouth
1 tsp. (5 mL) salt
1 tsp. (5 mL) freshly ground black pepper
1 tsp. (5mL) dried oregano
1 cup (240 mL) blanched, roughly chopped asparagus
1/2 cup (120 mL) grated Parmigiano-Reggiano cheese

Preheat the oven to 400°F (200°C). Butter the bottom and sides of the baking dish.

Melt 1 Tbsp. (15 mL) of the butter in a large saucepan over medium heat. Add the mushrooms and cook until they've released their moisture, about 5 minutes. Add another 1 Tbsp. (15 mL) of the butter and allow it to melt. Add the flour and whisk until the mixture is smooth, about 1 minute. Remove the saucepan from the heat and add the chicken stock, continuing to whisk the mixture. Add the cream and continue to whisk as you return the pan to the heat.

Allow the mixture to come to a simmer (light bubbles, not a rolling boil). Add the chicken to the mixture and cook for 1 minute. Remove from the heat and add the lemon juice, vermouth, salt, pepper and oregano. Add the asparagus to the pan and mix gently.

Place the entire mixture in the baking dish and top with the cheese. Bake for 25 minutes, or until the cheese is golden brown and the sauce bubbles gently.

hungarian chicken paprikash

This dish is passed down from the Hungarian side of my family. Velvety and rich, it's the perfect meal on a chilly night. For a slightly lighter version, you can use boneless and skinless chicken cuts. Serve this with broad egg noodles. Some white wine and gypsy music complement the meal!

3 large chicken legs with skin, bone in
2 chicken breasts with skin, bone in
4 Tbsp. (60 mL) olive oil
1½ cups (360 mL) chopped onions
salt and freshly ground black pepper to taste
3 tsp. (15 mL) Hungarian paprika
½ cup (120 mL) chicken stock
2 medium tomatoes, chopped
6 large button mushrooms, thinly sliced
1 large yellow bell pepper, finely chopped
½ cup (120 mL) white wine (optional)
2 Tbsp. (30 mL) sour cream (optional)

Preheat the oven to 400°F (200°C).

Rinse the chicken and pat it dry. Heat 3 Tbsp. (45 mL) of the oil in a medium skillet over medium-high heat. Add the onion and sauté for 4 minutes. Reduce the heat to medium-low. Add the salt, pepper and paprika and stir, cooking gently for 2 minutes. Do not let the paprika burn. Add the chicken to the pan and turn to coat the chicken evenly with the mixture. Transfer the chicken and mixture to the baking dish.

Deglaze the skillet with the white wine and add this to the baking dish. Top the chicken with the tomato. You may wish to add some more salt and pepper to taste at this point. Bake for 20 minutes. Cover the dish with foil and continue to bake for 20 minutes more.

In a large skillet add 1 Tbsp. (15 mL) oil and sauté the mushrooms and yellow pepper over medium heat for 4 minutes. Add the mixture to the baking dish, gently stirring it into the sauce. If you wish, deglaze the skillet with the white wine and add it to the baking dish. Continue baking, uncovered, for 20 minutes. You may serve the dish at this point or remove the chicken from the baking dish and pace on a platter tented with foil. Add the sour cream, if you wish, stirring it gently into the sauce. Serve immediately.

pesto-crusted chicken

The pesto creates a crust on the chicken breast, locking in the flavor. Try this with a Caesar salad and a crusty Italian roll. Bellisimo!

SERVES 2

2 boneless, skinless chicken breast halves
$1/4$ cup (60 mL) pesto sauce
2 Tbsp. (30 mL) Parmigiano-Reggiano cheese
freshly ground black pepper to taste

Preheat the oven on broil. Place the slotted tray in the baking dish.

Rinse the chicken and pat it dry. Combine the pesto with the cheese in a small bowl. Add the chicken and coat with the mixture. Place the chicken breasts on the slotted tray. Spread the remaining sauce on top of the chicken breasts. Broil for 12 to 15 minutes. Serve immediately.

roasted chicken and vegetables

If you love simple roasted chicken with potatoes and carrots, then this recipe is for you. It has the same flavor as a whole roasted chicken without the preparation time.

2 chicken thighs with skin, bone in
1 chicken breast with skin, bone in
¼ cup (60 mL) olive oil
juice of ½ lemon
1 Tbsp. (15mL) salt
1 tsp. (5 mL) freshly ground black pepper
1 tsp. (5 mL) dried oregano
1 tsp. (5 mL) dried thyme
1 medium potato
2 medium carrots

Preheat the oven to 400°F (200°C).

Rinse the chicken and pat it dry. Combine the olive oil, lemon juice, salt, pepper, oregano and thyme in a bowl. Add the chicken and coat with the mixture.

Cut the potato into quarters. Cut the carrots into 1-inch (2.5-cm) pieces. Add the vegetables to the chicken mixture and toss to coat.

Place all the ingredients in the baking dish. Make sure the chicken breast is placed skin side up. Roast for 35 minutes, tossing the vegetables every 15 minutes or so. Serve immediately.

chicken burgers

A great alternative to beef burgers. The addition of pork and pesto creates a moist and succulent burger. Serve them on crusty Italian rolls with your choice of condiments. If you only want to make two patties, you can freeze the other two. Just wrap them individually in wax paper and place in a freezer bag to freeze for another meal.

¹/₂ lb. (225 g) ground chicken
¹/₂ lb. (225 g) ground pork
¹/₂ small onion, minced
salt and freshly ground black pepper to taste
1 tsp. (5 mL) Italian seasoning mix
1 clove garlic, minced
1 egg
1 tsp. (5 mL) pesto sauce
1 Tbsp. (15 mL) finely grated Parmesan cheese

Preheat the oven on broil.

Mix all the ingredients together in a bowl. Form into 4 medium-sized patties, about 1 inch (2.5 cm) thick.

Place the patties on the slotted tray in the baking dish. Broil 8 minutes for medium done, turning once while cooking.

toaster roaster

Remember roast beef at Mom's? If you can't be there, you can still enjoy the dish. Making a roast isn't all that complicated. Have your butcher tie the beef loin at 2-inch (5-cm) intervals. (Remember to call your Mom and let her know you're eating well!)

1 2-lb. (900-g) boneless beef strip loin
1 Tbsp. (15 mL) salt
1 Tbsp. (15 mL) coarsely ground black pepper
1 Tbsp. (15 mL) dried oregano
2 cloves garlic, minced
3 Tbsp. (45 mL) olive oil
1 tsp. (5 mL) grainy mustard
2 tsp. (10 mL) lemon juice
1 Tbsp. (15 mL) dried thyme

Position the oven rack on its lowest setting. Preheat the oven to 425°F (220°C). Place the slotted tray in an inverted position in the baking dish.

Pat the meat dry with a paper towel. Combine the remaining ingredients in a bowl and mix well. Spread the mixture over the entire roast and transfer to the slotted tray, fat side up. Roast for 30 to 40 minutes, basting occasionally with the drippings.

Remove the meat to a platter and allow it to rest for 15 minutes before removing the strings and carving it. Carve the roast into 1/2-inch (.6-cm) slices and drizzle with the pan juices.

roasting beef

The bottom line is: do not overcook it, or you'll be left with a piece of shoe leather! Many experienced cooks know when a piece of meat is done simply by feeling it—a little poke tells them the degree of doneness. You can test for doneness by quickly pressing your finger into the meat. If the meat is soft, with a lot of give, it's rare. If it's got a little give, it's medium-rare. When firm it will be well done. Don't let it get hard though—that's when it's past being edible.

If you don't like the idea of the odd burnt finger, a meat thermometer is a good investment. Generally, for roast beef, the thermometer will read 115°F (46°C) for rare, 125°F (52°C) for medium rare and 135°F (57°C) for medium done.

hamburger! hamburger!

In colder climates, where I grew up, you can't really barbecue in the snow (although I've known some stalwart souls who do!). My Mom could always satisfy my craving for a burger by cooking these up in the toaster oven. Savory and delicious! Remember, you can always freeze two of the patties to have on hand for another occasion.

½ lb. (225 g) lean ground beef
½ lb. (225 g) ground pork
½ small onion, minced
salt and freshly ground black pepper to taste
1 tsp. (5 mL) dried oregano
1 clove garlic, minced
1 egg
1 tsp. (5 mL) olive oil
1 tsp. (5 mL) ground cumin

Preheat the oven on broil.

Mix all the ingredients together in a bowl. Form into 4 medium-sized patties, about 1 inch (2.5 cm) thick.

Place the patties on the slotted tray in the baking dish. Broil 8 to 10 minutes for medium, turning once during cooking.

bifsteaki hellas

The trick to a moist broiled steak is in the marinade, especially if it's a less expensive cut of meat. Greeks eat this with freshly squeezed lemon, which adds a clean, zesty flavor to the meal. For maximum effect, serve with Potatoes Opa! (page 56).

SERVES 2

2 steaks (ribeye or sirloin), 1½ inches (3.8 cm) thick
½ cup (120 mL) olive oil
½ cup (120 mL) lemon juice
salt and freshly ground black pepper to taste
1 Tbsp. (15 mL) dried oregano
½ lemon, quartered

Pat the steaks with a damp paper towel. Combine the olive oil, lemon juice, salt, pepper and oregano in a deep dish and add the steaks. Turn them a couple of times and place them in the fridge to marinate for at least 2 hours.

Preheat the oven on broil. Place the slotted tray in the baking dish.

Transfer the steaks to the slotted tray. Broil for about 5 minutes on each side.

Serve with lemon, squeezed over the steak just before eating.

steak house blues

Maybe it's not heart-friendly, but a girl or a guy has just got to have their steak sometimes. There's nothing like a good steak to make you feel special. This dish is the perfect match of robust flavor and extraordinary texture. OK, maybe the martini beforehand has something to do with setting the mood, but why go out when you can do it hassle-free in your own home? Hey! No tip required!

2 sirloin steaks about 1 1/2 inches (3.8 cm) thick
1 Tbsp. (15 mL) olive oil
2 tsp. (10 mL) salt and coarsely ground black pepper
2 Tbsp. (30 mL) blue cheese
1/4 cup (60 mL) red wine
1 Tbsp. (15 mL) brandy
1 tsp. (5 mL) butter

Preheat the oven on broil. Place the slotted tray in the baking dish.

Coat the steaks on both sides with olive oil. Press the salt and pepper into the oil and place the steaks on the tray. Broil for 7 minutes for medium-rare, turning once midway through cooking. Test for doneness. The steaks should be nicely browned on both sides.

When the steak is just about done, remove the pan and place 1 Tbsp. (15 mL) of blue cheese on top of each steak. Return to the broiler for 30 seconds. Remove the steaks and let rest on a warm plate. Tent a piece of foil over the top to keep them warm.

Carefully remove the slotted tray from the baking dish. Keep the broiler on. Add the red wine and brandy to the dish and give it a quick stir to remove any brown bits from the bottom. Return to the toaster oven and watch for the liquid to come just to a boil. Remove the dish, add the butter and stir to incorporate. Return to the oven for 30 seconds.

To serve, place a steak on each plate and pour the sauce over.

maria's meatloaf

SERVES 4

WITH LEFTOVERS

This is pure comfort food that goes really well with old-fashioned mashed potatoes. There's more than one meal here, but the beauty is you can use what's leftover for manly meatloaf sandwiches. Yum!

3/4 lb. (340 g) ground lean beef

3/4 lb. (340 g) ground pork

1 medium onion, minced

1 cup (240 mL) breadcrumbs

2 eggs, beaten

1/4 cup (60 mL) olive oil

1/2 cup (120 mL) finely grated
   Parmigiano-Reggiano cheese

1/4 cup (60 mL) grainy mustard

1/4 cup (60 mL) barbecue sauce

1 Tbsp. (15 mL) Italian spice mix

1 Tbsp. (15 mL) ground oregano

1 tsp. (5 mL) salt

1 tsp. (5 mL) freshly ground black pepper

1/4 cup (60 mL) ketchup

1/4 cup (60 mL) Dijon mustard

Place the oven rack on the lowest setting. Preheat the oven to 350°F (175°C). Lightly grease a 9- x 5- x 3-inch (23- x 12- x 7.5-cm) loaf pan.

Combine all the ingredients except the ketchup and Dijon mustard in a bowl, and mix to incorporate. Do not overprocess. Place the mixture in the loaf pan, mounding it. Lightly cover the meatloaf with a piece of foil to keep it from browning too quickly. Bake for 1 hour, removing the foil after the first 30 minutes. After 1 hour the meat should be firm to the touch and the meatloaf will have shrunk away from the sides of the loaf pan.

Combine the ketchup and Dijon mustard in a small bowl. Remove the meatloaf from the oven and pour the topping over the meatloaf. Return the meatloaf to the oven for 15 minutes to allow the topping to create a light crust.

Let the meatloaf sit for 15 minutes before cutting and serving.

slow-roasted beef short ribs

SERVES 4

I serve this with garlic-mashed potatoes and green beans. If there are leftovers, mix them with pasta for a light meal.

2 lbs. (900 g) beef short ribs, 2 inches (5 cm) thick and
    cut into 2- to 3-inch (5- to 7.5-cm) pieces
salt and freshly ground black pepper to taste
1 Tbsp. (15 mL) olive oil
1 small onion, minced
3 cloves garlic, minced
1 bay leaf
2 Tbsp. (30 mL) ground thyme
1½ cups (360 mL) red wine
2 cups (475 mL) beef stock
1 Tbsp. (15 mL) butter
2 Tbsp. (30 mL) grainy mustard

Place the oven rack on the highest setting. Preheat the oven on broil.

Pat the ribs dry and season them with salt and pepper. Oil the baking dish. Place the short ribs in the dish and broil the ribs, turning them to sear both sides. It should take about 5 minutes per side.

Change the heat setting to 350°F (175°C). Remove the dish from the oven and add the onion, garlic, bay leaf, thyme, wine and beef stock. Cover the baking dish with foil. Return to the oven and bake for 2 hours. The meat is done when it falls off the bone. Remove the ribs from the dish and place them in a bowl covered with foil.

Turn the oven setting to broil. Add the butter to the juice collected in the pan and whisk briskly. Return the dish to the oven for 1 minute. Remove and whisk again.

Add the mustard to the dish and whisk to blend well. Return the dish to the oven and allow the sauce to cook for 1 more minute. Pour the sauce over the short ribs and serve at once.

oven-roasted beef

This is the antidote to a cold winter's night. Serve in rustic bowls with crusty fresh bread.

SERVES 4

2-lb. (900-g) boneless beef chuck roast
1 tsp. (5 mL) salt
1 tsp. (5 mL) freshly ground black pepper
1 cup (240 mL) baby carrots
2 potatoes, cubed
1 10-oz. (284-mL) can condensed cream of tomato soup
2 cups (475 mL) water
1 cup (240 mL) red wine
1 Tbsp. (15 mL) ground thyme
1 Tbsp. (15 mL) ground oregano
1 beef bouillon cube, crumbled

Preheat the oven to 300°F (150°C).

Place the beef, salt, pepper, carrots, and potatoes in a 2-quart (2-L) casserole dish. Whisk the remaining ingredients in a bowl. Pour over the beef and vegetables. Cover with foil and roast for 2 hours, or until the beef is tender. Occasionally remove the foil to stir the vegetables and baste the meat. Serve immediately.

asian broil

Most flank steaks are too large for a toaster oven, so ask your butcher to cut it in half or into thirds, depending on how big the steak is. The longer you let this cut marinate, the more moist and tender it will be. If you have leftovers, you can thinly slice the steak and add it to stir-fried vegetables served over rice.

1 8-inch (20cm) flank steak
2 Tbsp. (30 mL) olive oil
1 cup (240 mL) soy sauce
1 Tbsp. (15 mL) oyster sauce
1/4 cup (60 mL) sweet sake or rice wine (optional)
2 green onions, sliced

Pat the flank steak dry. In a deep dish, combine the olive oil, soy sauce, oyster sauce, sake or rice wine and onions. Stir the marinade to combine all the ingredients and add the steak. Cover with plastic wrap and place in the refrigerator to marinate—overnight is best.

Preheat the oven on broil. Place the slotted tray in the baking dish.

Place the steak on the slotted tray. Discard the marinade. Broil for 5 minutes. Turn the steak and broil for 5 minutes more.

Remove the steak and let rest for 5 minutes before slicing. Slice the steak across the grain into 1/2-inch (1.2-cm) slices.

simple beef stew

The flavor of this stew is greatly enhanced if you wait until the next day to serve it. Patience is a virtue, my dear!

1/4 cup (60 mL) flour
3/4 tsp. (4 mL) salt
1/2 tsp. (2.5 mL) freshly ground black pepper
2 Tbsp. (30 mL) olive oil
2 lbs. (900 g) beef chuck, cut into 1-inch (2.5-cm) cubes
1 Tbsp. (15 mL) minced garlic
1 cup (240 mL) tomato juice
1/2 cup (120 mL) red wine
1/2 medium onion, cut in chunks
1 cup (240 mL) baby carrots
1 potato, peeled and cubed
1 stalk celery, coarsely chopped
2 Tbsp. (30 mL) Worcestershire sauce
1/2 envelope dry onion soup mix
1 cup (240 mL) water

Preheat the oven to 450°F (230°C).

Combine the flour, salt and pepper in a plastic bag. Add the beef and toss to coat. Heat the oil in a large skillet over medium heat. Add the beef. Cook, stirring occasionally, until the beef is browned on all sides.

Transfer the beef to a 2-quart (2-L) casserole dish. Add the remaining ingredients. Cover with foil and bake for 30 minutes. Reduce the temperature to 300°F (150°C) and simmer for 1 1/2 hours, until the beef is tender when pierced with a fork. Serve immediately or cool and refrigerate overnight, reheating for 1 hour at 300°F (150°C).

perfect pork chops

SERVES 2

A little entertaining to do after work but not a second to spare? Try these awesome chops and wait for the compliments to pour in. You can substitute lamb chops for the pork if you like. A simple tomato and red onion salad with some strategically placed steamed asparagus and you're off to the races. If this doesn't "wow" your guest, they're beyond hope and you, my dear, should find someone more worthy of your time and prowess in the kitchen! On your own tonight? I dare you not to eat the second chop!

2 Tbsp. (30 mL) olive oil
2 large butterfly pork chops, bone in
$1/2$ cup (120 mL) grainy mustard
$1/4$ cup (60 mL) chopped fresh cilantro or basil
$1/2$ cup (120 mL) grated Parmigiano-Reggiano cheese
freshly ground black pepper to taste

Preheat the oven to 350°F (175°C). Place the slotted tray in the baking dish.

Add 1 Tbsp. (15 mL) of the oil to a preheated large frying pan. When the oil is hot, but not smoking, add the pork chops and sear for 1 minute on each side. Remove the chops from the pan.

In a bowl, combine the mustard, cilantro or basil, cheese, black pepper and remaining 1 Tbsp. (15 mL) of olive oil. Distribute the mixture evenly over the chops, spreading it about $1/4$ inch (.6 cm) thick. Place the chops on the slotted tray and bake for 5 minutes. Reduce the heat to 325°F (165°C) and cook for another 15 minutes or until done. The crust should be golden brown and the juices should run clear. Serve immediately.

virginia bbq

I spent many a summer when I was growing up enjoying the taste of real southern barbecue. If I get to yearnin' for that taste but can't head down south, I cook up some of this.

SERVES 4

2-lb. (900-g) pork shoulder or Boston blade roast
½ large onion, thinly sliced
1 14-oz. (398-mL) can whole tomatoes
½ cup (120 mL) vinegar
2 Tbsp. (30 mL) Worcestershire sauce
2 Tbsp. (30 mL) water
1½ tsp. (7.5 mL) black pepper
1 Tbsp. (15 mL) salt
1½ Tbsp. (22.5 mL) sugar
1½ Tbsp. (22.5 mL) crushed red pepper

Move the oven rack to the lowest position. Preheat the oven to 325°F (165°C).

Line the baking dish with a large piece of foil (enough for the roast and its juices). Place the pork on the foil.

In a large mixing bowl combine the remaining ingredients. Stir to mix and break up the whole tomatoes. Pour the mixture over the pork. Fold the foil so that it covers the roast but doesn't seal it. Cook for 1½ hours, or until the meat falls away from the bone. Slice or mince the meat and serve with the sauce collected in the dish.

zingy pork chops
with tomato salsa

We cooked this one up one summer evening after a long day at work. It was so easy and delicious, it's become one of our favorites.

FOR THE PORK CHOPS:
2 boneless pork loin chops
1 Tbsp. (15 mL) chopped fresh thyme
1 Tbsp. (15 mL) chopped fresh basil
1 tsp. (5 mL) salt
1 tsp. (5 mL) ground black pepper
1 clove garlic, minced
juice of 1 lime
1 Tbsp. (15 mL) olive oil

Pat the chops dry. Mix the remaining ingredients in a bowl. Place the mixture in a container big enough to hold the chops, and add the chops to it, coating them in the mixture. Allow the chops to marinate for 30 minutes.

Preheat the oven on broil. Place the slotted tray in the baking dish. Place the chops on the slotted tray and cook for 5 minutes. Turn the chops and cook for 10 to 12 minutes more. Remove from the oven and let them rest for 5 minutes.

1 small tomato, chopped
½ small onion, minced
1 Tbsp. (15mL) balsamic vinegar
1 Tbsp. (15 mL) olive oil
1 garlic clove, minced
1 tsp. (5 mL) salt
1 tsp. (5 mL) ground black pepper
1 Tbsp. (15 mL) chopped fresh basil
juice from 1 lime

While the chops are cooking, combine all the salsa ingredients in a small bowl and set aside.

Serve the chops with some of the tomato salsa spooned over them.

bistro pork tenderloin

SERVES 2 C'est superbe! *The perfect accompaniment to a spinach salad or sour cream mashed potatoes.*

1 pork tenderloin, about 10 oz. (285 g)
salt and freshly ground black pepper to taste
1 Tbsp. (15 mL) olive oil
½ cup (120 mL) lemon juice
1 clove garlic, minced
1 Tbsp. (15 mL) dried oregano
1 Tbsp. (15 mL) Spike seasoning

In a bowl combine the pork with the remaining ingredients. Marinate for 20 minutes.

Preheat the oven on broil. Place the slotted tray in the baking dish.

Place the tenderloin on the tray and broil for 20 minutes, turning once halfway through. Baste with the drippings in the pan. Let the tenderloin sit for 5 minutes before slicing into 1-inch-thick (2.5-cm) pieces.

Serve immediately with the sauce collected in the dish.

honey-roasted spareribs

A sweet and sour, sticky delight! Serve with steamed green beans and some boiled baby potatoes drizzled with olive oil.

1 tsp. (5 mL) minced garlic
1 cup (240 mL) packed light brown sugar
1 cup (240 mL) honey
¼ cup (60 mL) cider vinegar
¼ cup (60 mL) Worcestershire sauce
1 Tbsp. (15 mL) salt
2 tsp. (10 mL) ground ginger
1 tsp. (5 mL) hot pepper sauce
2 racks baby pork spareribs, about 2 lbs. (900 g)

Preheat the oven to 350°F (175°C).

Combine the garlic, brown sugar, honey, vinegar, Worcestershire sauce, salt, ginger and pepper sauce in a large bowl and mix well. Cut the ribs to fit into the baking dish without touching the sides. With a pastry brush or spoon, coat the ribs with the marinade. Place the coated spareribs in the baking dish and pour 1 cup (240 mL) of the marinade over the ribs. Roast for 40 minutes. Add the remaining marinade and roast for an additional 40 minutes.

damn good lamb shanks

Making a dish that calls for adding red wine means I can open up a good bottle (you never want to cook with inferior wine) and enjoy a glass while the dish gets some too! I use a premium Cabernet Sauvignon when I make these shanks and I always serve them with rich mashed potatoes.

¼ tsp. (60 mL) ground cumin
¼ tsp. (60 mL) ground coriander
1 Tbsp. (15 mL) dried thyme
1 tsp. (5 mL) salt
½ tsp. (2.5 mL) freshly ground black pepper
3 large cloves garlic
4 medium spring lamb shanks
2 Tbsp. (30 mL) olive oil
½ small onion, finely chopped
1 cinnamon stick
1 whole clove
1 bay leaf
2 Tbsp. (30 mL) all-purpose flour
1 cup (240 mL) chicken stock
1 cup (240 mL) dry red wine
salt and cracked black pepper to taste

Preheat the oven to 400°F (200°C).

Combine the cumin, coriander, thyme, salt and pepper in a small bowl. Roughly cut two of the garlic cloves into 4 slices each. Make 2 incisions in each shank with a small knife. Stuff with a sliver of the garlic. Dredge the shanks in the spice and herb mixture.

Heat a large frying pan over medium heat, add 1 Tbsp. (15 mL) of the oil and sear 2 of the shanks for about 2 minutes, turning often, until golden brown. Transfer to the baking dish. Repeat with the remaining 1 Tbsp. (15 mL) of olive oil and the 2 remaining shanks.

Mince the third garlic clove. Add the minced garlic, onion, cinnamon stick, clove, bay leaf and any of the leftover herbs and spices from the seasoning mixture to the baking dish.

Sprinkle the lamb with flour, turning the shanks to coat them evenly. Roast uncovered for about 20 minutes.

Reduce the heat to 375°F (190°C). Add the chicken stock, wine and cracked black pepper to taste. Cover tightly with foil and cook for about 45 minutes.

Remove the dish and baste the lamb with the juices from the pan. If there is not enough liquid, add another 1/2 cup (120 mL) of red wine. Seal tightly and continue to cook for another 30 minutes. The lamb is done when the meat is tender and almost falling off the bone. The sauce should have a thick consistency. Season with more salt and pepper, if desired.

it's all greek to me leg of lamb

SERVES 4

What can I say . . . Greeks know lamb. If you have any left-overs, the meat makes a wicked sandwich. Have your butcher cut the bone close to the meat to ensure it fits in the baking dish.

3 ½ lbs. (1.6 kg) leg of baby lamb, bone in
4 cloves garlic, sliced in half
1 cup (240 mL) extra virgin olive oil
juice of 1 lemon
salt and freshly ground black pepper to taste
½ cup (120 mL) roughly chopped fresh parsley
1 Tbsp. (15 mL) roughly chopped fresh sage
2 Tbsp. (30 mL) dried oregano
1 tsp. (5 mL) Italian seasoning mix
16 baby potatoes, peeled

Using a sharp knife, make 8 small punctures in the lamb, stuffing each one with half a garlic clove.

Place the lamb in a large bowl. In a smaller bowl, whisk the oil, lemon juice, salt, pepper, parsley, sage, oregano and Italian seasoning mix together. Pour over the lamb. Cover and refrigerate overnight, occasionally turning the lamb in the marinade.

Preheat the oven to 425°F (220°C).

Cut a large piece of foil that will completely enclose the lamb and the marinade. Place the foil in the baking dish. Place the lamb in the center and pour the marinade over. Roll the foil down along the sides of the baking dish, allowing the lamb to cook uncovered. Roast for 30 minutes.

Reduce the heat to 350°F (175°C). Baste the lamb and add the potatoes to the dish. Tightly seal the foil, being careful not to let the marinade out. Roast for 1 hour and 30 minutes.

Open the foil package and remove the potatoes to a warm dish. Continue to roast the lamb uncovered for 30 minutes more.

Remove the lamb to a warm platter and cover with a tent of foil. Pour the juices from the pan into a bowl. Set the oven on broil.

Return the potatoes to the baking dish and broil for 15 minutes as the lamb rests.

Skim off the fat from the top of the juice before serving with the lamb and potatoes.

baked scallops and mushrooms
in garlic sauce

SERVES 4

This makes a lovely appetizer but I like it as a main course with a simple salad. If there are leftovers, toss them with some fresh pasta or rice. Serving with a glass of crisp Sauvignon Blanc works well in either case.

3 Tbsp. (45 mL) olive oil
½ lb. (225 g) pound medium white button mushrooms
¾ lb. (340 g) sea or bay scallops
¼ cup (60 mL) all-purpose flour
¼ cup (60 mL) dry white wine
3 Tbsp. (45 mL) fine dry breadcrumbs
2 Tbsp. (30 mL) minced onion
1 Tbsp. (15 mL) minced fresh parsley
2 cloves garlic, minced or pressed
pinch crushed red pepper flakes
salt and freshly ground black pepper to taste

Preheat the oven to 350°F (175°C). Coat the baking dish with 1 Tbsp. (15 mL) of the olive oil.

Remove the stems from the mushrooms and set aside both the stems and caps.

Rinse the scallops in cold water and pat them dry with paper towels. Toss the scallops with the flour. Arrange the scallops and the mushroom caps in a single layer in the baking dish. Add the wine, being careful to pour it at the side of the dish.

Finely chop the mushroom stems and mix them with the breadcrumbs, onion, parsley, garlic, pepper flakes, salt and pepper. Sprinkle this mixture over the scallops and mushrooms. Drizzle with the remaining 2 Tbsp. (30 mL) of olive oil.

Bake for 30 minutes, until the mushrooms are soft and the scallops are cooked through. Serve immediately.

broiled salmon

This dish has an oriental flare with the addition of five-spice powder, which is readily available in the spice section of your local grocery. I love this served with blanched asparagus topped with a citrus oil and salt.

SERVES 2

2 salmon fillets, about 3 inches (7.5 cm) wide and
   2 inches (5 cm) thick
2 Tbsp. (30 mL) olive oil
juice of one lime
2 Tbsp. (30 mL) five-spice powder
salt and freshly ground pepper to taste

Preheat the oven on broil. Insert the slotted tray into the baking dish.

Pat the fillets dry. In a large bowl, combine the oil, lime juice, 1 Tbsp. (15 mL) of the five-spice powder, salt and pepper. Add the fillets to the marinade and let sit for 5 minutes. Transfer the salmon to the slotted tray in the baking dish. Sprinkle the remaining five-spice powder over the salmon.

Broil for 15 to 20 minutes, until the salmon is cooked and golden brown on top. Serve immediately.

southern catfish

Down-home cookin' without all the grease. This fish is out-standing. It's moist, flavorful and sure to please. I crush the crackers and almonds by placing them in a resealable plastic bag and gently hammering it ... really gets the stress of the day out! You can substitute Dover sole or whitefish fillets if you can't find catfish. Serve with mango salsa, tartar sauce or simply a slice of lemon.

$3/_4$ cup (180 mL) crushed whole-wheat crackers
$3/_4$ cup (60 mL) roasted slivered almonds, crushed
1 tsp. (5 mL) salt
1 Tbsp. (15 mL) freshly ground black pepper
1 Tbsp. (15 mL) Italian seasoning mix
$1/_4$ cup (60 mL) chopped fresh cilantro
1 egg
1 egg white
2 catfish fillets (without skin or bones)

Preheat the oven to 350°F (175°C). Coat the slotted tray evenly with butter-flavored cooking spray.

Place the crackers and almonds, salt, pepper, Italian seasoning mix and cilantro in a plastic bag. Shake to mix. Beat the egg and egg white together in a bowl. Dip the fish fillets in the egg mixture, coating them evenly. Place one fillet at a time in the bag of dry mixture. Shake to evenly coat the fillets.

Place the fillets on the slotted tray. Lightly spray the tops of the fillets with cooking spray. Bake for 20 minutes, or until crispy on the outside and tender and flaky on the inside. When tested with a fork, the fish should be firm but not dry.

just for the halibut

There's a famous Italian restaurant in Vancouver that makes the most amazing halibut. This is my version of that meal. I try to use fresh fish whenever I can, but with halibut, frozen will do. Serve this with creamy whipped potatoes.

SERVES 4

4 halibut steaks
1 medium onion, thinly sliced
½ cup (120 mL) sliced white button mushrooms
¼ cup (60 mL) chopped green bell pepper
1 tsp. (5 mL) garlic
½ cup (120 mL) dry white wine
2 tsp. (10 mL) vinegar
1 tsp. (5 mL) salt
½ tsp. (2.5 mL) black pepper
¾ cup (180 mL) stewed tomatoes, drained
¼ cup (60 mL) minced fresh parsley
2 Tbsp. (30 mL) butter
4 lemon wedges, for garnish (about half a
    medium lemon)

Preheat the oven to 350°F (175°C). Pat the fish dry with paper towels.

Spray the baking dish with a vegetable cooking spray. Place the onions on the bottom of the dish. Place the fish on top of the onions. In a bowl, combine the mushrooms, bell pepper, garlic, wine, vinegar, salt, pepper, tomatoes and parsley. Pour over the fish. Dot with the butter.

Bake for 20 to 25 minutes, or until the fish begins to flake. The cooking time will depend on the thickness of the steaks. Serve with the lemon wedges.

crab-stuffed poblano chiles
with mango salsa

Be careful when working with chiles. They not only pack a bite but the oil from them can remain on your hands and cause a nasty "spice burn" if you don't take precautions—like wearing rubber gloves. To find fresh poblano chiles you may have to go to a Latin or South American grocery store. You can substitute bell peppers for the poblanos and add some chili pepper spice (just a touch!), but the dish won't have quite the same bite or smoky flavor.

FOR THE MANGO SALSA:

1 cup (240 mL) chopped peeled mango
⅓ cup (80 mL) chopped red bell pepper
2 Tbsp. (30 mL) chopped fresh cilantro
1 Tbsp. (15 mL) balsamic or white wine vinegar

Combine the mango, bell pepper, cilantro and vinegar in a small bowl and stir well. Cover and chill.

FOR THE STUFFED CHILES:

3 Tbsp. (45 mL) grated fresh Parmigiano-Reggiano cheese
1 tsp. (5 mL) dried oregano
1 tsp. (5 mL) Dijon mustard
⅛ tsp. (.5 mL) freshly ground black pepper
1 12-oz. (340-mL) container of ricotta cheese
1 12-oz. (340-mL) can quartered artichoke hearts, drained
1 6-oz. (170-mL) can lump crabmeat, drained
4 5-inch fresh poblano chiles, halved lengthwise
    and seeded
cilantro sprigs, for garnish

Preheat the oven to 350°F (175°C).

In a bowl, combine 2 Tbsp. (30 mL) of the Parmigiano-Reggiano cheese with the oregano, mustard, pepper and ricotta cheese. Stir in the artichokes and the crabmeat. Divide the mixture evenly among the chile halves, and sprinkle with the remaining 1 Tbsp. (15 mL) of cheese.

Place the stuffed chiles in the baking dish and bake for 30 minutes, until lightly browned.

Serve with the mango salsa and garnish with cilantro sprigs.

italian cod

My partner's children went on a fishing expedition and caught a lingcod of gigantic proportions. While the fish may not be one of the most beautiful (frankly, it's ugly!) the meat is tender and sweet. That catch (and all that fish) inspired me to make this dish.

1/4 cup (60 mL) butter
1 small onion, chopped
1 green bell pepper, chopped
1 tsp. (5 mL) dried basil, crumbled
1 14-oz. (398-mL) can tomatoes, drained, chopped
salt and freshly ground black pepper to taste
1 1/2 lbs. (680 g) lingcod fillets or haddock
2 cups (475 mL) grated mozzarella cheese

Preheat the oven to 350°F (175°C). Butter the baking dish.

Melt the butter in a large saucepan over medium-high heat. Add the onion, bell pepper and basil and sauté until the vegetables are tender, about 10 minutes. Stir in the tomatoes. Season with salt and pepper and cook until thick, stirring constantly, about 5 minutes.

Arrange the fish in the prepared dish. Pour the sauce over top and sprinkle with the mozzarella. Bake until the fish is cooked through and the top is golden brown, about 25 minutes.

steamy sea bass

The lightness of the cooking method is balanced by the rich flavor of this fish. I serve it over a bed of spiced couscous with dried fruit.

2 6-oz. (170-g) portions Chilean sea bass
¼ cup (60 mL) olive oil
1 tsp. (5 mL) ground coriander
¼ cup (60 mL) lemon juice
2 Tbsp. (30 mL) minced garlic
½ cup (120 mL) chopped roasted tomatoes (see page 60)
5 fresh thyme sprigs
salt and freshly ground black pepper to taste

Preheat the oven to 350°F (175°C).

Cut a piece of foil large enough to enclose the fish and place the foil on the baking dish. Place the fish in the center of the foil and fold up the sides of the foil a little to create a lip. Add the remaining ingredients to the fish. Tightly seal the foil, enclosing the fish.

Bake for 25 minutes. The fish will steam in the foil. Be careful not to scald yourself with the escaping steam when removing the fish from the foil. Serve immediately.

cannelloni with curves

Serves 3

Vroom! This dish rocks. It's a parcel of cheesy delight that melts in your mouth. Serve with roasted asparagus for an added touch of color.

2 Tbsp. (30 mL) olive oil
¼ cup (60 mL) finely chopped onion
1 clove garlic, finely chopped
½ tsp. (2.5 mL) salt
½ tsp. (2.5 mL) dried parsley
¼ cup (60 mL) chopped roasted green pepper
   (see page 61)
¼ cup (60 mL) chopped roasted tomatoes (see page 60)
1 egg, beaten
¼ cup (60 mL) ricotta cheese
¼ cup (60 mL) cottage cheese
¼ cup (60 mL) grated Parmigiano-Reggiano cheese
¼ cup (60 mL) goat cheese
2 cups (475 mL) crushed tomato sauce
6 oven-ready cannelloni
¼ cup (60 mL) water
¾ cup (180 mL) grated Parmigiano-Reggiano cheese

Preheat the oven to 350°F (175°C).

Heat the oil in a saucepan over medium heat; add the onion, garlic, salt and parsley and sauté until the onion is soft, about 4 minutes. Remove from the heat and add the roasted pepper and tomatoes. Set aside to cool.

Mix the egg, ricotta, cottage cheese, ¼ cup (60 mL) Parmigiano-Reggiano and goat cheese in a bowl. Add the vegetable mixture to the cheese mixture and blend together.

Spread half of the tomato sauce in the bottom of the baking dish. Fill the cannelloni with the cheese mixture. Place the cannelloni in a single layer on top of the sauce. Cover with the remaining tomato sauce and drizzle the water over all.

Cover with foil and bake for 45 minutes, or until the pasta is tender.

Serve topped with the remaining $^3/_4$ cup (180 mL) Parmigiano-Reggiano cheese.

tomato and eggplant pasta bake

SERVES 4

Chop the eggplant as small or as large as you like. This meal is very easy to prepare, especially if you've got some leftover plain pasta in the fridge. You may substitute zucchini for the eggplant if you wish. This recipe can easily be cut in half, but you'll need to use a smaller baking dish.

4 cups (950 g) cooked fusilli pasta
2 cups (475 mL) Maria's Tomato Sauce (see page 75)
1 cup (240 mL) chopped roasted eggplant (see page 62)
1 cup (240 mL) Parmigiano-Reggiano cheese
$\frac{1}{2}$ cup (120 mL) breadcrumbs
6 oz. (170 g) goat cheese
2 Tbsp. (30 mL) chopped fresh parsley

Preheat the oven to 350°F (175°C).

Combine the pasta with the tomato sauce and eggplant. Transfer to the baking dish. Sprinkle the Parmigiano-Reggiano cheese and the breadcrumbs over the top of the pasta. Slice the goat cheese into six pieces and place it on top of the pasta.

Bake for 20 minutes. Sprinkle the top with parsley and serve immediately.

ABOVE: simple beef stew (page 107)

PREVIOUS PAGE: broiled salmon (page 119)

ABOVE: maria's meatloaf (page 102)

FOLLOWING PAGE: tomato lasagna (page 132)

ABOVE: good old macaroni and cheese (page 134)
PREVIOUS PAGE: yemista (mint stuffed vegetables) (page 70)

ABOVE: cambi cheese cookies (page 146)
FOLLOWING PAGE: fruit crisp (page 142)

speedy classic lasagna

I use oven-ready noodles just because it's so much easier!
They work great and I can't tell the difference from conven-
tionally cooked packaged noodles. Serve this with a salad
and crusty bread. For serving those who are really famished,
you could easily cut the lasagna into 4 generous pieces.

SERVES 6

2 Tbsp. (30 mL) olive oil
1 small onion, chopped
1 clove garlic, chopped
1 large carrot, minced
$^1/_2$ lb. (225 g) lean ground beef
$^1/_2$ lb. (225 g) ground pork
2 cups (475 mL) pasta sauce of your choice
$^1/_4$ cup (60 mL) chopped fresh parsley
1 Tbsp. (15 mL) Italian seasoning mix
$^1/_2$ cup (120 mL) chicken stock or water
$^1/_2$ lb. (225 g) ricotta cheese
$^1/_2$ lb. (225 g) cottage cheese
$^1/_2$ package (150 g) baby spinach, roughly chopped
12 oven-ready lasagna noodles
$^1/_4$ cup (60 mL) shredded mozzarella cheese
$^1/_4$ cup (60 mL) grated Parmigiano-Reggiano cheese

Preheat the oven to 350°F (175°C).

Heat the oil in a saucepan over medium heat. Add the
onion, garlic and carrot and cook until tender, about
5 minutes. Add the meat and cook until browned. Drain
off the fat. Stir in the pasta sauce, parsley, Italian seasoning and chicken stock or water. Simmer the mixture for
4 to 5 minutes.

Combine the ricotta and cottage cheese with the spinach.

Spread $\frac{1}{4}$ of the meat sauce in the bottom of a 2-quart (2-L) casserole dish.

Top with 4 noodles. Add another $\frac{1}{4}$ of the meat sauce and $\frac{1}{2}$ of the cheese mixture. Top with 4 more noodles, $\frac{1}{4}$ of the meat sauce and the remaining cheese mixture. Finish with the last 4 noodles and the remaining meat sauce. Sprinkle the top with the mozzarella and Parmigiano-Reggiano.

Cover the baking dish with foil. Bake for 30 minutes. Remove the foil and bake for another 20 minutes. Let the lasagna stand for 10 minutes before serving.

seafood lasagna

Seafood makes a lovely twist to classic lasagna. If you can find spinach oven-ready noodles, do try them—the green color really adds to the dish. Instead of tomato sauce try a cream sauce for a different effect.

SERVES 4 TO 6

2 eggs, beaten
2 cups (475 mL) ricotta cheese
1/3 cup (80 mL) chopped fresh dill
1/2 cup (120 mL) whipping cream
2 cups (475 mL) pasta sauce of your choice
12 oven-ready lasagna noodles
1/2 lb. (225 g) small cooked shrimp
1/2 lb. (225 g) small cooked scallops
3 cups (720 mL) shredded mozzarella cheese

Preheat the oven to 350°F (175°C).

In a bowl, whisk together the eggs, ricotta cheese and dill. In a separate bowl, stir together the cream and pasta sauce.

Spread 1/2 cup (120 mL) of the pasta sauce in a 3-quart (3-L) casserole dish. Top with 4 lasagna noodles. Spread 1/2 of the ricotta mixture over the noodles. Cover with 1/3 of the remaining pasta sauce. Sprinkle with 1/2 of the shrimp and scallops and 1 cup (240 mL) of the mozzarella cheese.

Top with 4 more lasagna noodles. Add the remaining ricotta mixture, 1/3 of the pasta sauce, the remaining shrimp and scallops and 1 cup (240 mL) of the mozzarella cheese. Finish with the remaining noodles, pasta sauce and cheese.

Cover and bake for 45 to 50 minutes. Remove from the oven and let stand at least 15 minutes before serving.

tomato lasagna

This is my family's favorite. It's rustic, yet light, and it smells heavenly. If you're also having salad and bread you could get away with serving smaller portions to 6 people. Leftovers reheat well for lunch the next day.

FOR THE SAUCE:

2 Tbsp. (30 mL) olive oil

1 medium onion, finely chopped

2 garlic cloves, minced

2 cups (475 mL) crushed tomato sauce

2 Tbsp. (30 mL) tomato paste

1/2 cup (120 mL) white wine

1 bay leaf

2 Tbsp. (30 mL) Italian seasoning mix

salt and freshly ground black pepper to taste

1 tsp. (5 mL) sugar

Heat the oil in a large saucepan over medium heat. Add the onion and cook until it is translucent, about 4 minutes. Add the garlic, cooking and stirring for 2 minutes. Stir in the tomato sauce and cook for another 2 minutes. Add the tomato paste, wine, bay leaf, Italian seasoning mix, salt, pepper and sugar. Reduce the heat to medium-low and simmer for 30 minutes.

FOR THE LASAGNA:

12 oven-ready lasagna noodles

2 medium bocconcini cheeses, diced

1 cup (240 mL) grated Parmigiano-Reggiano cheese

8 large basil leaves

1 Tbsp. (15 mL) olive oil

Preheat the oven to 375°F (190°C).

Spoon $1/4$ of the tomato sauce on the bottom of the dish. Lay 4 noodles over the sauce. Add another $1/4$ of the tomato sauce over the noodles. Scatter $1/2$ of the basil and bocconcini over the sauce. Sprinkle with $1/3$ of the Parmigiano-Reggiano cheese. Repeat with another layer of noodles, pasta sauce, basil and cheeses. Finish with the final 4 noodles, then the remaining pasta sauce and Parmigiano-Reggiano. Drizzle the top with the olive oil and cover the dish with foil.

Bake for 20 minutes. Remove the foil and bake for another 25 minutes, until the top is golden and the cheese is bubbling. Let the lasagna sit for 5 minutes before cutting and serving.

good old macaroni and cheese

This is an old standard in the arena of comfort foods, but this version gets a slightly new twist with the addition of roasted tomatoes—you can substitute sun-dried tomatoes from the jar if you wish. Try it served with some steamed broccoli drizzled with olive oil and sea salt.

2 cups (475 mL) macaroni
2 Tbsp. (30 mL) butter
2 Tbsp. (30 mL) flour
1½ cups (360 mL) warm milk
pinch salt
1 tsp. (5 mL) Dijon or grainy mustard
1 cup (240 mL) grated sharp Cheddar cheese
½ cup (120 mL) roughly chopped roasted tomatoes
   (see page 60)
½ cup (120 mL) grated Parmigiano-Reggiano cheese

Preheat the oven to 350°F (175°C). Lightly butter a 2-quart (2-L) casserole dish.

Cook the macaroni according to package directions. Melt the butter in a saucepan over medium heat. Add the flour and cook, stirring constantly, for 3 to 4 minutes. Gradually whisk in the milk and continue to cook and stir until it is thickened. Season to taste with salt. Remove from the heat and stir in the mustard, cheese and tomatoes. Add the macaroni and stir to coat.

Transfer to the casserole and top with the Parmigiano-Reggiano cheese. Bake for 30 minutes, until the top is golden brown. Serve immediately.

notes

notes

desserts

"a real treat"

"one word . . . decadent"

"smile with anticipation"

"perfect with afternoon
tea or coffee"

bruschetta of pears and apples
with warm crème fraîche

One word . . . decadent! Vanilla beans are incredible—their aroma alone lets you know this is going to be good. They are a bit of a luxury, however, so savor this dessert. Crème fraîche can now be found in the dairy sections of fine food stores. To make it at home, mix together equal parts of sour cream and whipping cream. If you like, you can substitute Devon cream or vanilla ice cream for the crème fraîche but if you use ice cream, don't warm it first!

4 vanilla beans
1 cup (240 mL) sugar
1 pear, quartered and cored
1 Granny Smith apple, quartered and cored
1 cup (240 mL) ice wine or a late harvest Riesling wine
6 ½-inch-thick (1.2-cm) slices sourdough bread
¼ cup (62 mL) unsalted butter
1 cup (240 mL) crème fraîche
6 fresh mint leaves

In a food processor or blender, purée 1 vanilla bean and the sugar. Cut each pear and apple half into 4 to 6 chunks and place in a large bowl. Sprinkle the sugar on top, pour in the wine, and stir. Cover with plastic wrap and let macerate for at least 20 minutes.

Preheat the oven to 400°F (200°C). Butter 6 ovenproof ramekins.

Spread each slice of bread with butter. Place a piece of bread, butter side up, in each ramekin. Top with the fruit mixture. Bake for 15 to 20 minutes, until golden.

Warm the crème fraîche in a small skillet over very low heat. Split the remaining 3 vanilla beans in half. Drizzle each serving with warmed crème fraîche and top with half a vanilla bean and a mint leaf.

clafouti

Clafouti is one of the best ways to enjoy cherries in season. When they're not in season, you can substitute canned. Serve it warm or chilled.

SERVES 6 TO 8

3 eggs
1½ cups (360 mL) sugar
¼ cup (60 mL) flour
1 oz. (28 mL) Kirsch or other cherry-flavored liqueur
2 cups (475 mL) whipping cream
2 lbs. (900 g) fresh cherries, stemmed and pitted

Preheat the oven to 375°F (190°C). Lightly butter a 2-quart (2-L) casserole dish.

Whisk together the eggs, sugar, flour, liqueur and cream in a deep bowl.

Fill the casserole dish with the cherries. Pour the custard over the cherries. Bake for 40 minutes, or until the custard is firm.

carrot loaf with
lemon cream cheese icing

This is a real treat with afternoon coffee or tea. The lemon cream cheese icing is a perfect complement to the carrot loaf, but if you're watching calories, it's just as delicious without it.

½ cup (240 mL) olive oil

2 eggs

1 tsp. (5 mL) vanilla extract

2 Tbsp. (30 mL) applesauce

³/₄ cup (180 mL) sugar

1 cup (240 mL) all-purpose flour

¼ tsp. (1.2 mL) baking soda

³/₄ tsp. (4 mL) baking powder

½ tsp. (2.5 mL) ground cinnamon

³/₄ tsp. (4 mL) pumpkin pie spice

¼ cup (60 mL) chopped pecans

¼ cup (60 mL) grated coconut

1 cup (240 mL) grated carrots

Preheat the oven to 350°F (175°C). Butter and flour a 9- x 5- x 3-inch (23- x 12- x 7.5-cm) loaf pan.

Combine the oil, eggs, vanilla, applesauce and sugar in a large bowl and mix well.

In a second bowl, sift together the flour, baking soda, baking powder, cinnamon and pumpkin pie spice. Add the dry ingredients to the wet and mix with a whisk to incorporate. Be careful not to overblend the batter. The mixture should look smooth.

Fold in the pecans, coconut and carrots. Pour the mixture into the prepared loaf pan and bake for about 25 to 35 minutes, or until a toothpick inserted in the center comes out clean. Cool on a wire rack before icing.

lemon cream cheese icing

½ cup (120 mL) cream cheese, softened to
    room temperature
finely grated zest of 1 lemon
1 Tbsp. (15 mL) lemon juice
¼ tsp. (1.2 mL) vanilla extract
⅓ cup (80 mL) whipping cream
¼ cup (60 mL) icing sugar

MAKES APPROXIMATELY 1 CUP (240 mL)

Whisk together the cream cheese, ½ of the lemon zest, lemon juice, vanilla, whipping cream and icing sugar, beating until smooth.

Spoon over the cooled carrot loaf. Garnish with the remaining lemon zest.

fruit crisp

This, of course, is a dessert made for vanilla ice cream. It's so easy to prepare and provides maximum flavor. The sweetness of the fruit and the nuttiness of the crumble—you've just got to have it!

2 cups (480 mL) sliced apples
1 cup (240 mL) frozen blueberries
1 cup (240 mL) quick-cooking rolled oats
2/3 cup (160 mL) brown sugar
1/2 cup (120 mL) flour
1 tsp. (5 mL) ground cinnamon
1/4 tsp. (1.2 mL) salt
1/4 tsp. (1.2 mL) ground nutmeg
1/2 cup (120 mL) butter, melted

Preheat the oven to 400°F (200°C). Lightly butter the baking dish.

Place the apples or berries in the baking dish.

In a medium bowl, combine the oats, brown sugar, flour, cinnamon, salt and nutmeg. Stir to mix. Add the butter and stir until crumbly. Spoon the mixture on top of the fruit. Bake for 30 minutes, or until the apples are tender and the top is bubbly.

lemon squares

These remind me of sunny days, bright blue skies and having tea with my nanny. They still make me smile with anticipation.

FOR THE BASE:
1 cup (240 mL) butter, softened
½ cup (120 mL) sugar
2 cups (240 mL) flour

Preheat the oven to 350°F (175°C).

Combine the butter, sugar and flour in a bowl, mixing well to incorporate the ingredients. Press the mixture into the bottom of the baking dish. Place in the oven and bake for 20 minutes, or until the edges just turn brown.

FOR THE TOPPING:
4 eggs
2 cups (240 mL) sugar
½ tsp. (2.5 mL) vanilla extract
½ cup (120 mL) flour
1 tsp. (5 mL) baking powder
¼ cup (60 mL) lemon juice
2 Tbsp. (30 mL) lime juice
grated zest of 1 lemon

In the same bowl, beat the eggs. Slowly add the sugar, then the vanilla, flour, baking powder, lemon and lime juice and lemon zest. When the crust is baked, pour the egg mixture over the crust.

Return to the oven and bake an additional 20 to 25 minutes, until set. Cool in the pan before cutting into squares.

everything but the
kitchen sink cake

This is so easy—simple ingredients and no special mixing required. The trick with the icing is to make sure the cream cheese is soft but still cold when you beat it. If you choose not to make the frosting, you can finish the cake with a sprinkling of icing sugar.

FOR THE CAKE:

2 cups (475 mL) all-purpose flour

2 cups (475 mL) sugar

½ cup (120 mL) vegetable oil

1 cup (240 mL) chopped walnuts

1 14-oz. (398-mL) can apple pie filling

2 eggs

2 tsp. (10 mL) baking soda

1 tsp. (5 mL) salt

1 tsp. (5 mL) ground cinnamon

1 tsp. (5 mL) vanilla extract

¾ cup (180 mL) raisins

Preheat the oven to 350°F (175°C). Butter and flour the baking dish.

Place all the ingredients in a large bowl and mix with a spoon. Pour the batter in the baking dish or a 9- x 11-inch (22.5- x 27.5-cm) baking pan. Bake for 50 minutes, until a toothpick inserted into the center of the cake comes out clean. Cool on a wire rack.

6 oz. (170 g) cream cheese, softened but still cold
$^1/_4$ cup (60 mL) butter, softened
1 tsp. (5 mL) vanilla extract
2 cups (480 mL) icing sugar

Beat the cream cheese, using an electric hand mixer, in a large bowl. Add the butter and mix well with the cream cheese. With the mixer on low, add the vanilla and icing sugar. Beat until smooth. Ice the cake when it has cooled completely.

cambi cheese cookies

MAKES ABOUT
1 DOZEN
COOKIES

These little cookies take the place of a heavy dessert and can substitute for a cheese course at the end of a meal. You'll have to do them in 2 batches, 6 at a time (or you can freeze half the dough to bake on another occasion).

½ cup (120 mL) crumbled Cambozola cheese, chilled
¼ cup (60 mL) unsalted butter, at room temperature
¼ tsp. (1.2 mL) freshly ground black pepper
2 tsp. (10 mL) granulated sugar
½ cup (120 mL) all-purpose flour
¼ cup (60 mL) coarsely chopped fresh walnuts, toasted
15 dried cranberries

Preheat oven to 350°F (180°C).

Combine the cheese, butter, pepper and sugar in a bowl and beat with an electric hand mixer until blended. Don't overmix: some larger crumbles of the cheese should still be evident in the dough. Using a wooden spoon, gently stir in the flour and nuts.

Form the dough into 1-inch (2.5-cm) balls and arrange in the ungreased baking dish. Using your fingers, lightly press down on the balls until they are ¼ inch (.6 cm) thick. Press a dried cranberry into the center of each cookie. Bake until slightly golden on the bottom and edges, about 20 to 25 minutes. Cool on a rack. Store in an airtight container in the refrigerator for up to 1 week.

notes

notes

notes

index

promotional message

DeLonghi is proud to be a promotional partner for *Toasted: The New Toaster Oven Cookbook*. DeLonghi has a long history of making premium bake & broil ovens, also known as toaster ovens. These compact ovens offer many attributes that conventional ovens do not have. They are smaller so they are faster to pre-heat and save power. As you will find while making many of the delicious meals in this book, the cooking results are wonderful.

Bake & broil ovens continue to evolve. Convection cooking is becoming more popular as we all have less time to prepare food. Convection baking reduces the cooking time by approximately 30%. It provides the best results when used for cakes, cookies and other foods that need to rise or require very even heat. Not only does convection baking help to bake better, but this feature allows you to dehydrate food so you can lock the freshness in your favorite fruits and vegetables.

There are many options on the market when you are selecting a toaster oven. You can choose traditional baking or the convection format. In recent years digital controls, two-hour timers and interior lights have been added to some models. Certain models even have a rotisserie. Some bake & broil ovens are slightly larger in size, but not in the amount of counter space they occupy. Small roasts and full meals can be cooked in these ovens.

One very important bonus of the smaller energy saving style of oven is that there is less to clean than a large oven. Less surface means less time spent doing the worst job in the kitchen—oven cleaning! A porcelain enamel interior such as Durastone by DeLonghi or others can be very helpful in clean-up. Slide out crumb trays help to take care of the oven floor without a lot of mess. (Try finding that on a large oven.)

When you want to purchase a new oven, some variations you can look for are: porcelain enamel interior versus painted enamel, high cavity (allowing you to fit a roast) or low cavity, oven light, convection option, rotisserie and dedicated functions for specific types of food, such as pizza. Higher end models even have chrome exteriors and a stylish design that will complement your kitchen. Whatever you choose, you will enjoy using your bake & broil oven to make the delicious recipes in this book.

about the author

Maria Hauschel learned from her mother early in life that each meal is special even if there's not much time to prepare it. In her family everyone lives to eat, and this passion was passed from mother to daughter along with a knack for creating mouthwatering recipes for the toaster oven.

The inspiration for *Toasted: The New Toaster Oven Cookbook* came when she realized that using a toaster oven to cook held great appeal for empty nesters like her parents as well as students and young couples such as Maria and her fiancé.

It is Maria's business to be aware of such demographics. She runs her own public relations consulting firm, Zuzu Communications. The company is named after her mischievous cat who sometimes thinks she's a dog. The name means "little bug" in Greek.

A native of London, Ontario, Maria has spent time in Toronto and San Francisco. From 1983 to 1987, she attended the University of Western Ontario, and then completed a Certificate in Public Relations at Ryerson Polytechnic University. Maria now resides in Vancouver, but still calls her parents in Ontario every day. She considers them her "rock," and the most passionate people she knows.

A self-confirmed information junkie, Maria has a voracious appetite for the news (papers, television and the Internet). She also loves cooking magazines, good wine, a great hockey game and shopping for black boots, of which she owns ten pairs.